**New Directions for
Community Colleges**

Arthur M. Cohen
EDITOR-IN-CHIEF

Florence B. Brawer
ASSOCIATE EDITOR

Carrie B. Kisker
MANAGING EDITOR

Community College Student Affairs: What Really Matters

Steven R. Helfgot
Marguerite M. Culp
EDITORS

Number 131 • Fall 2005
Jossey-Bass
San Francisco

COMMUNITY COLLEGE STUDENT AFFAIRS: WHAT REALLY MATTERS
Steven R. Helfgot, Marguerite M. Culp (eds.)
New Directions for Community Colleges, no. 131

Arthur M. Cohen, Editor-in-Chief
Florence B. Brawer, Associate Editor

NEW DIRECTIONS FOR COMMUNITY COLLEGES (ISSN 0194-3081, electronic ISSN 1536-0733) is part of The Jossey-Bass Higher and Adult Education Series and is published quarterly by Wiley Subscription Services, Inc., A Wiley Company, at Jossey-Bass, 989 Market Street, San Francisco, California 94103-1741. Periodicals Postage Paid at San Francisco, California, and at additional mailing offices. POSTMASTER: Send address changes to New Directions for Community Colleges, Jossey-Bass, 989 Market Street, San Francisco, California 94103-1741.

SUBSCRIPTIONS cost $80.00 for individuals and $170.00 for institutions, agencies, and libraries. Prices subject to change. See order form in back of book.

EDITORIAL CORRESPONDENCE should be sent to the Editor-in-Chief, Arthur M. Cohen, at the Graduate School of Education and Information Studies, University of California, Box 951521, Los Angeles, California 90095-1521. All manuscripts receive anonymous reviews by external referees.

New Directions for Community Colleges is indexed in Current Index to Journals in Education (ERIC).

Microfilm copies of issues and articles are available in 16mm and 35mm, as well as microfiche in 105mm, through University Microfilms Inc., 300 North Zeeb Road, Ann Arbor, Michigan 48106-1346.

CONTENTS

Editors' Notes

For higher education, this is a time that is, perhaps, like no other. Political and cultural conflicts are emerging on campuses across the country, college operating costs and tuition are increasing, and funding for higher education is static or declining in many states. At the same time, demands for colleges and universities to prove their worth and demonstrate both their educational effectiveness and their cost-effectiveness have grown into a nationwide accountability movement.

With open door admissions policies, a history of providing access and opportunity for a college education to those who traditionally have had neither, and a commitment to keeping costs low and providing remediation to those who need it, community colleges have had to work exceptionally hard to demonstrate their efficacy and respond to demands for accountability. Too often, despite their very different mission, community colleges have had to respond to the same demands and use the same measures of success as four-year colleges and universities.

For institutions of higher education, the most common measure of success is degree completion, although some critics argue that this is not always appropriate. The measure of degree completion is even less appropriate for community colleges, whose students' backgrounds, educational and career goals, and attendance patterns are widely diverse. Thus, for community colleges the questions of what needs to be measured, of what really matters, are very real.

Looking at what really matters becomes a point of departure from traditional measures of accountability in community colleges. Informed by a growing focus on the idea of student success that emerged in the early to mid-1990s, and even more by the emergence of the learning college movement shortly thereafter, community colleges have started to ask what students really need and want, if students are learning, and if, at the end of the day, students are achieving success as a result of their community college education. These are the outcomes for which community colleges should be held accountable. To achieve this kind of accountability, however, community colleges must be able to define success and learning in meaningful ways, and more importantly, must be able to use these definitions to measure learning and success.

An inevitable consequence of defining and measuring learning and success is discovering which programs, services, and learning experiences help achieve the desired results and which do not. Student affairs professionals in the community college have always been student-centered, always believed in the value of the work that they do, and always known that they make a difference in the lives of students. Now they are focusing on identifying which programs and services really matter and gathering data to guide the decision-making process.

This volume of *New Directions for Community Colleges* is designed to help answer the question of what really matters in community college student affairs. In preparation for this volume, we wanted to know what community college leaders thought about student affairs in their institutions. In the summer of 2004 we sent a survey to a national sample of community college chancellors and presidents, senior student affairs officers, deans of students, and leaders of national associations. We asked questions that would help us understand perceived threats and opportunities, the role and reputation of the division of student affairs in the institution, and the current and potential connection of the work of student affairs professionals to student learning and success. Complete survey results are included in the Appendix to this volume, but we will highlight a few here.

Seventy-three percent of the community college leaders surveyed predicted that the role of student affairs in the community college would increase because of the emphasis on student learning, changing student and faculty demographics, and the need to support new groups of students (e-learners and dual enrollment high school students, for example). As one president noted, "Student affairs is a vital part of the college, and I don't think that will change over time; the way in which services are delivered may change and the mix of services may change, but there will be a significant role to be played."

When presented with a list of thirteen potential challenges to the community college, these same leaders identified lack of stability in resources and funding, the focus on student learning and student success, and enrollment growth or fluctuation as the major challenges that could threaten their institutions and student affairs. From the same list, respondents also identified these challenges with the potential to change student affairs at their institutions: the emphasis on accountability and the need to quantify results, enrollment growth, shifting student demographics, and the focus on student engagement, student learning, and student success. In responding to an open-ended question about what would most strengthen student affairs at their institutions, respondents identified thirty-one items. The following appeared most frequently: more staff development, additional staff and funding, more involvement with instruction, and a better understanding of student affairs across the institution. In general, there was a high level of agreement among respondents over the main challenges facing student affairs, as well as a sense that student affairs divisions must—now more than ever—use their resources to support the institution's mission, offer quality programs that increase the chances students will succeed, and demonstrate in a concrete manner that student affairs programs add value to students, faculty, staff, and the institution.

Authors used these survey results to guide the development of their chapters and to identify topics that mattered most. In Chapter One, Steven Helfgot defines key terms in the student affairs field, discusses the core values that have defined and continue to define the profession, and identifies major issues facing community college student affairs professionals. The chapter sets the stage for the rest of the volume by asking student affairs professionals to look at their work in terms of its contribution to student learning and success while remaining true to their underlying professional values.

In Chapter Two, Martha Oburn discusses the importance and the power of evidence in community college student affairs practice. In this era of accountability, passion for our work, commitment to students, and a belief in the effectiveness of the services we provide are insufficient. In student affairs, as in all other aspects of institutional life, data must drive the work. Time, energy, and resources have to be devoted to those programs and services that are shown to make a difference and that help achieve desired outcomes.

Establishing a culture of evidence does not mean that student affairs professionals have to abandon those services that have so long characterized their practice in the community college, but it does mean that they must take a critical look at traditional support services, use data to identify programs and services that really matter, and allocate resources to support those programs. In Chapter Three, Marguerite Culp examines traditional support services in the community college, describes how they must be focused and strengthened to support student learning and success more effectively, and provides examples of best practices in community college student affairs.

As we assert throughout this volume, student learning is the core mission of the community college. Student learning includes classroom instruction, but it encompasses much more than that. Supporting student learning requires taking a holistic, integrated approach to supporting student success, which can only happen when student affairs professionals actively and fully partner with their academic affairs colleagues. In Chapter Four, Paul Dale and Tonya Drake discuss the importance of partnerships between academic and student affairs divisions and explore their value to learning-centered community colleges.

If community college student affairs programs are truly data-driven, supportive of student learning, and targeted at student success, what role will theory and research play in the evolution of programs and services? In Chapter Five, Dawn Person, Pilar Ellis, Caryn Plum, and Debra Boudreau identify emerging theories and research findings that practitioners can use to strengthen career counseling programs and support services for all students, especially those from populations historically underrepresented in higher education.

In many ways, it is easy to talk about what ought to be the work of student affairs, about what really matters, and why it matters. We can articulate principles and make persuasive arguments, but it is much more difficult for practitioners to put principles into action. Chapter Six, written by Marguerite Culp, offers some clear and simple guidelines for putting ideas into practice and doing more of what matters. As well, in Chapter Seven, Carrie Kisker points student affairs professionals toward resources that they can use to learn more about an institutional focus on student learning, translating student development theory into practice, and assessing student learning outcomes.

These are challenging times for community colleges and student affairs professionals, but challenges often have opportunities embedded in them. By holistically focusing on student learning, promoting student success, and placing institutional priority on those services and activities that really matter, student affairs professionals can take advantage of the opportunities embedded in today's challenges. Our hope is that this volume will allow readers to understand better the challenges faced by community college student affairs professionals. More importantly, we hope it will allow them to take advantage of the opportunities that accompany these challenges to support and strengthen community college student affairs programs that really matter.

Steven R. Helfgot
Marguerite M. Culp
Editors

STEVEN R. HELFGOT *is vice chancellor for student development and community affairs at the Maricopa Community Colleges in Arizona.*

MARGUERITE M. CULP, *formerly senior student affairs officer at Austin Community College in Texas, is now executive director of Solutions-Oriented Consulting in Florida.*

1

In a professional world characterized by change, uncertainty, and increased pressure to demonstrate that what they do really matters, community college student affairs professionals need clear definitions, a shared understanding of critical professional issues, and professional values that are consistent and congruent. This chapter provides those definitions and identifies core values and major issues for student affairs professionals in community colleges.

Core Values and Major Issues in Student Affairs Practice: What Really Matters?

Steven R. Helfgot

Professional life in the community college can often feel like a perpetual roller-coaster. The reasons for this are varied. First, community colleges are responsive institutions. They respond to the needs of changing populations and the changing workforce. They respond to the ebb and flow of the local economy. They respond to the demands of multiple stakeholders: from students, to families, to legislators, to local business leaders. Second, community colleges see their status and reputation fluctuate, sometimes wildly, most often through no fault of their own. When colleges respond to community needs for a trained workforce, for example, they are often criticized for not transferring more students to the university, yet when they concentrate on the transfer function, they may be criticized for ignoring community or workforce needs. Finally, community colleges are highly susceptible to changes in state funding or support. In one year they might be the darling of a state legislature, fully funded and able to expand programs and services. But just as quickly other priorities emerge, and community college funding drops, programs and services are cut back, and students are unable to receive the quality, flexible education they deserve.

Student affairs professionals ride this roller-coaster with all of their colleagues. Often, however, these professionals ride yet another roller-coaster, one that is specific to their particular mission and objectives. Again, there are several reasons for this instability. First, the status of student affairs in community colleges is less stable than that of other important administrative units. For example, the need for academic affairs in higher educational institutions is never questioned. Everyone agrees that academics are central to the college mission. And although there may be ongoing discussions about academic quality, the teaching and learning process, and teaching methods, there are never discussions (nor should there be) about whether teaching and learning should occur. The same is true—though to a lesser degree—for business or administrative affairs. Though the academic community will argue about how big such a unit ought to be and about how responsive it is, there are no questions about its necessity. Buildings must be maintained. Staff and bills need to be paid. Technology has to be operated and maintained.

For student affairs, however, the situation always seems to be in flux. To be sure, there are times when the functions provided by student affairs are embraced by the institution, and student affairs professionals are welcomed as full partners in the educational enterprise. At other times, however, student affairs is viewed as a drain on institutional resources or "fluff" that adds little or no value to the enterprise. Sadly, student affairs professionals too often exacerbate this situation. Though passionate about their work and deeply committed to students and student success, they are perceived to lack a core, a set of constants that define their profession and its practice. Student affairs professionals are not always able to articulate clearly what they do, why they do it, and why it matters. This then leads others to ask those very questions.

Because community colleges exist in a dynamic world where change is ever-present, this questioning may not be entirely surprising. It is, however, problematic. The student affairs profession does not need to reinvent itself every few years, and should not need to defend itself with every shift in direction or focus. Yet too often, student affairs professionals feel the need to do both. But that can change.

After defining some key terms, this chapter discusses the student affairs profession's core values, which are deeply embedded in its history and closely aligned with the community college mission. It then identifies major issues that seem to be almost universally occurring in community colleges across the country. In doing so, this chapter provides a conceptual anchor for understanding student affairs practice in the community college and an opportunity for student affairs professionals and their colleagues, both inside and outside the community college and the profession, to understand "what really matters."

Definitions

Some of the misunderstandings about student affairs, perpetuated by both those outside and in the profession, are a result of confusion about titles, vocabulary, lexicon, and definitions. As responses to the survey conducted for this volume document (see the Editors' Notes for more information about this survey), we call ourselves too many different things. Sometimes these labels are interchangeable, and at other times they mean entirely different things. At the risk of adding to this confusion, but in the hope of providing some clarity, I suggest the following definitions.

Student Affairs. In its broadest sense, student affairs is the discipline practiced by all of those who work in the general field and its numerous specialties. It has a body of knowledge, a professional literature, a long-established professional philosophy ("The Student Personnel Point of View"; see American Council on Education, 1983), a theoretical base (student development theory), and a set of commonly recognized jobs and functions. Generally, student affairs focuses on all things related to the student and the student's life in the college but outside the classroom. Student affairs also refers to the administrative unit of the college in which the services, programs, functions, and activities with this focus are housed.

Student Services. Student services are those programs, services, and activities provided or made available to students by a college's division of student affairs. These often include, but are not necessarily limited to, outreach and recruitment, admissions and records, assessment, advisement, orientation, financial aid, academic support programs, counseling, career planning and placement, and student activities, athletics, health and wellness, and college safety. Because many see the provision of these services as the essential function of the division in which they are housed, they often choose to name that division *student services* as opposed to *student affairs*. Others suggest that there is more to the work of this division than the mere provision of services, and that by using a service-oriented label, we both limit and define too narrowly the focus and work of this area. The argument is perhaps interesting to those in the profession and to educational scholars, but to many it is just a source of confusion . . . and that's not the end of it!

Student Affairs Professionals. Student affairs professionals are those who work in and provide the programs and services enumerated in the preceding paragraphs. They have a wide range and variety of titles that reflect both rank and the specialty area in which they work.

Student Development. This term entered the professional lexicon in the late 1960s and early 1970s and has come, over time, to mean two things. First, it has become the theoretical and conceptual underpinning of the student affairs profession. Student development theory describes how students change, grow, and develop as a result of the college experience. Though student development theory continues to expand, the two most common foundations are psychosocial theory, which is essentially about the development of identity, and cognitive developmental theory, which is about how students make meaning out of information and experience. (See Chapter Seven for resources providing more information about these theories or their application to practice.)

Student affairs professionals have widely embraced student development theory, and in doing so have made student development an intentional goal. Indeed, student development as a *goal* is the second meaning of the term. Because this goal has been so widely embraced across the profession, many have chosen it as the designated name for the division, as opposed to *student affairs* or *student services*. Once more, the debate may be interesting and the sentiments noble, but confusion is often the outcome.

Student Success. Over the last decade, student success has entered the professional vocabulary. Today there are student success programs, student success centers, and offices of student success with their own deans and directors. A definition of student success seems obvious . . . and simple: the achievement by a student of his or her chosen goal. Student success, however, is more complicated than that, as is shown later in this chapter, and as is repeatedly demonstrated throughout this volume.

Core Values in Community College Student Affairs

The student affairs profession emerged in the traditional, four-year college environment and thus predates the widespread growth and expansion of community colleges. Many of the core values that guide the profession were first articulated in its founding statement, the 1937 "Student Personnel Point of View" (American Council on Education, 1983) and still guide the profession today. Community colleges have both adopted and adapted those values in documents such as the 1984 and 2004 *Traverse City Statements* (Keyser, 1984; National Council on Student Development, 2004), which articulated a more contemporary role for community college student affairs. And although student affairs *practice* may differ in the community college environment and change with more diverse students, these core values remain a constant guide to practice. The core values that follow, although not a comprehensive list, reflect the history of the student affairs profession as well as the realities in today's community colleges.

A Commitment to the Whole Student. Community colleges are primarily focused on their academic missions . . . as they should be. Students, after all, come to the college to learn. Today, this focus is greater than ever, and in many community colleges, being learning-centered has become a dominant theme. Community college student affairs professionals should be and are committed to student learning, both inside the classroom and out. However, they also need to remind their colleges and their colleagues that, in the words of "The Student Personnel Point of View," it is the obligation of the college "to consider the student as a whole" (American Council on Education, 1983, p. 76). Student affairs professionals know and should help their institutions to understand that students are whole people. They have lives, relationships, and multiple roles. Community college faculty and staff must work to develop students' affective traits, not just their cognitive ones, and provide opportunities for learning and development in that domain.

Put simply, it is important for students to learn philosophy in college, but it is equally important for them to use their college experience to develop a philosophy. This is the essence of student development. Being in college is about developing an identity, a sense of purpose, and a sense of self; it is about developing life and career goals, meaning, and purpose. Today, it is about developing soft skills that employers find increasingly important: interpersonal skills, communication skills, leadership skills, and the ability to work as part of a team. These are the abilities that student affairs professionals provide to students in settings ranging from academic advising sessions to human development classes, from leadership training activities to career planning programs.

Recognition and Appreciation of Individual Differences. Community colleges are currently the most diverse institutions in higher education, and are becoming ever more diverse. Community college students have different learning styles, personality types, and abilities, as well as differing levels of academic success and preparation. Beyond that, on many community college campuses there is remarkable ethnic and socioeconomic diversity. There are students younger than traditional college age, and there are senior citizens. On many campuses there are significantly more women than men. There are new Americans and non-native speakers of English. There are students with advanced placement and dual enrollment credits, who take a full courseload and move through the college in significantly less than two years. And there are students who take only one class a semester, requiring a decade or more to finish their community college program. There are students who work full-time, students working multiple jobs, and students who do not work at all. As well, there are students who are fully supported by their families while pursuing their education, and others who must fully support their *own* families while going to school.

Community college student affairs professionals who are doing "what really matters" to help ensure that students are successful recognize and value this universe of individual differences, and customize programs and services accordingly. These professionals know that one size does not fit all. Some programs and services meet the needs of a large percentage of students, and some could assist large numbers with a few small modifications to their basic design. In other cases, a program or service is specially designed to meet the needs of a small group of students. By designing programs and services in this way, community college student affairs professionals recognize and appreciate individual differences and demonstrate that all students matter.

A Commitment to Facilitating Student Development, Success, and Learning. As noted, *student development* entered the lexicon in the late 1960s, while *student success* emerged in the 1990s; the focus on *student learning* followed shortly thereafter. Yet these more contemporary terms are really embodiments of enduring student affairs values. To "assist the student in developing to the limits of his potentialities" (American Council on Education, 1983, p. 3) is at the core of "The Student Personnel Point of View." And more than three decades ago, as student affairs practice was emerging in the community college, Matson (1972) indicated that community college student affairs professionals should focus on integrating their work "into the central activity of any educational institution, namely learning" (p. 178).

Providing Quality Services to Meet Student Needs. From the first delineation of services in "The Student Personnel Point of View" to contemporary discussions of those programs today, student affairs professionals have always emphasized the importance of offering an array of services to meet student needs. Community college student affairs professionals have reaffirmed that commitment, and enhanced it in a variety of ways. For example, in the 1984 *Traverse City Statement,* community college leaders acknowledged the need to "maximize student success through services such as . . . assessment . . . placement, orientation, academic advising, career planning, counseling, financial aid, and job and transfer placement" (Keyser, 1984, p. 36). Today more than ever before, student affairs leaders emphasize the provision of quality services to meet the needs of diverse students as well as the importance of empirically verifying that quality. In the words of the National Council on Student Development (2004), community college student affairs professionals "must demonstrate that efforts to serve students actually do make a difference in academic success, retention, and persistence, as well as [in] cognitive and affective development" (p. 2).

In today's environment, providing quality services to meet student needs includes providing support, consultation, and service to staff and faculty who are, for many community college students, the principal if not the only point of contact. Indeed, "student development professionals should collaborate with faculty and staff on how to enhance student learning inside and outside the classroom" (National Council on Student Development, 2004, p. 9).

A Belief in the Power and Richness of the Out-of-Class Environment. Whether it is called the cocurriculum or the extracurriculum, whether it is named student activities, student life, or student leadership, the fundamental belief that life outside the classroom can provide opportunities for student learning and development and contribute to student success has been and continues to be a core value in community college student affairs. This value is reflected in the League for Innovation in the Community College's 1987 statement, "Assuring Student Success in the Community College," which reaffirmed "the causal relationship between student involvement on campus and student success" (p. 4).

A Commitment to Providing Access and Opportunity. This core value emerges as much from traditional community college sources as from traditional student affairs values. The egalitarian mission of community colleges is well-known, as is their open door admissions policy, which provides not only a gateway to higher education for many students but also a "second chance" for many others. A commitment to providing access and opportunity is both embraced and advocated by community college student affairs professionals, and it is integrated into student affairs in programs ranging from outreach and recruitment to adult reentry services, from mandatory assessment and placement to advising and orientation. Providing access and opportunity is, in many ways, the mantra of community college student affairs.

The Changing Face of the Community College

Although the student affairs profession's core values remain consistent and always guide practice, practice itself changes over time as new issues and trends emerge in community colleges and new and different groups of students arrive on community college campuses. The following trends have emerged over the past few years, and each uniquely affects student affairs practice.

Expanded Focus on Student Learning. Community colleges have always been student-centered institutions with faculty who are first and foremost teachers. Over the years, however, the discourse surrounding the focus on student learning has changed. A generation ago, community colleges were often called *teaching institutions,* a name that then gave way to colleges focused on the *teaching and learning process.* Today, increasingly, they are described as *learning colleges,* which focus primarily on student learning rather than teaching. This focus has particular implications for student affairs professionals because the concept of student learning is often extended to include learning outside the classroom (American College Personnel Association, 1996). This new focus requires student affairs professionals to think and act in new ways. Advisers, counselors, financial aid officers, orientation and student life directors, as well as other student affairs professionals, are asking themselves what students can and should learn as a result of participating in their programs, services, and activities. To answer those questions they are developing learning objectives and outcomes for their programs and looking for ways to assess if those outcomes have been achieved.

Focus on Student Success. Student success emerged as a focus first for student affairs professionals in the community college (Helfgot and Culp, 1995), and later for the community college as a whole. Student success encompasses more than student learning; it also incorporates students' ability to achieve realistic goals and to apply and use what they have learned. Student success means, for example, that a student who has earned a degree or certificate in a particular field is able to obtain and perform successfully in a job in that field, or that a student who completes the requirements for university transfer is, in fact, able to transfer to and compete effectively at the university.

The implications of the focus on student success are clear for those who work in student affairs. Career counselors, for example, must establish relationships with faculty in career programs. Through those relationships, counselors can provide students preparing to enter the workforce with the opportunity to participate in activities such as résumé writing workshops and practice interviews. Similarly, student affairs professionals who work in transfer centers or articulation offices should work with faculty and administrators responsible for transfer programs to provide students with the assistance they need to transfer successfully and on time.

Use of Outcomes and Measures for Nontraditional Students. Currently there are vigorous discussions about the appropriateness of two of the most common outcome measures used by community colleges—number of degrees and certificates awarded and number of students who transfer to a university—to a nontraditional student population. The essence of this discourse is that many community college students seek neither degrees nor certificates. Rather, they have other objectives and use community colleges to design or customize their own educational programs. For example, many community college students can be characterized as *serial learners:* students already in the workforce who come to the community college seeking a specific course or package of courses, often from different programs and disciplines. When they finish the courses they leave the college. Serial learners usually do not earn a degree or certificate, but they meet an important goal and the college successfully meets their needs. Frequently, these students will repeat this pattern a number of times; thus the term *serial learners.*

Other community college students have begun to use the institution as a sort of graduate school. It is not uncommon for students to complete a baccalaureate degree in a particular field or in general studies and then return to the community college to pursue training in a specific career—for example, nursing, computer programming, or teacher certification. This is, perhaps, the most sophisticated example of how students use the community college to design and package an educational program that fits their unique needs and circumstances. In sum, these enrollment patterns present new challenges to advisers, counselors, and financial aid officers, who need new models of practice to meet the needs of nontraditional students.

Baccalaureate Degrees. Community colleges are becoming more active in providing baccalaureate degrees, sometimes on their own, and sometimes in partnership with four-year colleges and universities. Some community colleges are building full-service university centers on their campuses, others are offering baccalaureate degrees in select areas, and still others are becoming full baccalaureate-granting institutions. Whatever the form, this trend represents a tremendous shift for those working in student affairs in the community college. Advisers need new conceptual and structural models for students who will stay at the institution through the baccalaureate. Those in student activities, with responsibility for student government and student leadership, must think about how to structure these programs to include both two-year and four-year students. Professionals working with academic honors societies have similar issues to address. In all cases, although the student affairs professionals involved will surely have the skills they need to do this work, the challenge will be in developing appropriate content and workable structures to accommodate both baccalaureate and nonbaccalaureate students.

These emerging trends in the community college have the potential to affect student affairs practice, as well as all parts of the institution, in profound ways. It is imperative, therefore, that community college student affairs professionals know their core values so they are better equipped to face both these trends and the resulting issues for the profession.

Major Issues in Community College Student Affairs

Many of the issues that confront community colleges emerge at a particular time and in a particular set of circumstances, and can often be addressed and effectively dealt with. At other times, issues will disappear as the circumstances that brought them to the surface change. Conversely, several issues in community colleges are persistent and require continued attention over time. The important issues that follow fall into the latter category, and are consistent problems that must be examined, reexamined, and addressed over time. This list is not exhaustive, but it reflects the views of the community college leaders surveyed for this volume. (Again, see the Editors' Notes for a description of the survey, and the Appendix at the back of this volume for complete survey results.)

How Does Student Affairs Help Shape and Support the Institution's Central Mission? Multiple factors contribute to—and at times limit—the influence student affairs professionals have in shaping and supporting their college's central mission. In the survey conducted for this volume, community college student affairs professionals were asked several questions, the answers to which allow us to at least infer the role of student affairs in shaping the central mission of the college: student learning and success.

In our survey, senior student affairs officers were asked to whom they report. Roughly 85 percent responded that they reported directly to the chancellor or president. Clearly having "a seat at the table"—in this case the president's table—provides student affairs administrators with a voice in discussions and decisions that help shape institutional mission and priorities.

Another survey question asked respondents how they thought the role of student affairs in their institution would change in the next five to ten years. Nearly three-quarters (73 percent) thought student affairs' role would increase. The percentage of college presidents who believed that the role of student affairs would increase in their institution was even greater, with 79 percent indicating that they thought this would be the case.

These responses clearly suggest that student affairs professionals are well positioned to help shape the core mission of the college. Actually doing so, however, requires more than a seat at the table; it requires a broad and deep understanding of students and their needs, an ability to describe those needs in both qualitative and quantitative terms, and the ability to demonstrate that student affairs professionals can meet those needs and make a difference in the institution itself.

Because attitude is often reflective of behavior, our survey asked community college student affairs professionals about their attitudes toward student learning and success. Survey participants were given a list of fourteen major challenges to community college student affairs practice and asked to rank them from most to least important. Among those listed was "student learning and student success." Almost 38 percent of the respondents ranked this as the number one challenge. Nearly 64 percent ranked it in the top three.

Of all the challenges to community college practice, only "the lack of stability in funding" came close to this particular issue, with 60 percent ranking funding stability among the top three challenges to community college student affairs practice. Of course, being committed to student learning and success is not in itself a challenge, but finding the tools to operationalize and validate that commitment is an issue for many. It could be inferred that community college student affairs professionals are engaged in supporting student learning and student success but challenged by the need to develop measurable learning and developmental outcomes, measure those outcomes, and develop programs and services to improve student success.

How Do Student Affairs Professionals Add Value to the Institution's Work? The notion of adding value seems at first blush to be a bit archaic, the language of another time. Yet on reflection, it makes great sense in terms of what we want student affairs to do. The overriding institutional goals—student learning and student success—define to a great degree the work of the faculty. Yet student affairs professionals add value by supporting student learning and providing a variety of programs and services intentionally designed to help students be more successful. One senior student affairs officer commented on our survey, "Our services and programs are being viewed more and more within the light of what we do to support student learning"; another observed that "student services is inextricably linked with instruction and part of student success."

With some exceptions, community college divisions of student affairs look pretty similar. They comprise services and programs that are easily recognized and familiar to most in higher education. Each is important, meets some set of student needs, and it may be argued, adds value to the work of the college. However, as Chapter Three suggests, student affairs professionals need to reexamine how their programs and services help students and should assist the college in fostering student learning and ensuring student success. For example, community college student affairs professionals should set learning goals for students as they interact with programs and services in order to contribute to a pervasive culture of learning in the institution. As well, in the design and delivery of programs and services, there should be a consideration of student goals—both large and small—and an attempt to help students successfully meet those goals as they engage with the program or service. Finally, student affairs professionals should make sure that the programs and services they offer contribute in a unique way to the institution's most important goals, student learning and success.

Do Student Affairs Organizational Structures Meet the Needs of Today's Community College Students? The organizational structure of community college student affairs offices is largely derivative of those in place at four-year colleges and universities when "junior" colleges were founded. These divisions included many of the services described in "The Student Personnel Point of View," which was appropriate because, in those early days, two-year and four-year college students were much more alike than they are today.

In today's community colleges, however, students do not always reflect their university counterparts, and are often much more diverse. Given this diversity of students and academic and vocational goals, student affairs professionals need to continuously examine and reexamine the array of services they offer, the organization of those services, and the ways in which they are delivered. Are they the right services for the mix of students in the institution? Are they appropriate to the diversity of students on campus and the diversity of student goals? Do they connect meaningfully to student and institutional goals? Is student affairs organized in ways that are both student- and learning-centered? Do programs and services actively contribute to student learning and development, and do they promote student success?

Is Student Affairs Sufficiently Outcome- and Data-Driven? In his 2004 address to the National Council for Student Development, Terry O'Banion, longtime president of the League for Innovation in the Community College, asked community college student affairs professionals to respond to the same question he has continually posed to community college leaders: "Do the programs and services you offer make a difference to students, and how do you know that they do?" Kay McClenney, director of the Community College Survey of Student Engagement, believes that for community colleges, the anecdote is the coin of the realm, and urges community college educators to prove the effectiveness of their work not by anecdotes alone but by presenting data based on previously defined goals and outcome measures for individual students, specific groups, and the student body as a whole (McClenney, 2004).

Becoming more data-driven is a special challenge for student affairs professionals because many believe that what they do is difficult to measure (which, to some extent, is true). In this era of increased accountability and competition for resources, however, that explanation will not carry much weight, mainly because it is possible to do more. We can define learning outcomes. We can define student success. We can identify elements of student development that can be measured. We can take into consideration traditional measures such as retention, persistence, certificate and degree completion, and transfer. We can look at programs and services to determine what relationships exist between student participation and the various measures of student success. Finally, we can define new and nontraditional outcomes and determine if there is a relationship between student services and student goal achievement. As the National Council on Student Development states, "The role for accountability and the imposition of external mandates will require systematic assessment for all student development programs and services." (2004, p. 2).

How Can Student Affairs Provide Quality Services in an Environment of Constantly Shifting Demographics? Community college students are ever changing. In a publication for the National Association of Student Personnel Administrators, Helfgot (1998) concluded, "New students come to our campuses in waves, and while the students in each wave are new to higher education, that may be the only characteristic they share"(p. 3).

Yet as student affairs professionals, our services tend to remain more constant than our students, even though there is no guarantee that what works for one group of students will work with another. Student affairs professionals need to constantly watch for shifting demographics and other changes in the student body, and then assess the effectiveness of programs and services *for specific groups or categories of students*. As McClenney (2004) suggests, practitioners must "break down the data by race and ethnicity, income, gender, and age" and then "ask the right questions of the data" (p. 14). Quality and appropriate services may remain relatively constant across groups of students, but they do not *always* apply across racial, gender, or age groups. Rather than assume that all programs and services will benefit all students, student affairs professionals must learn how to serve a diverse student body.

How Can Student Affairs Compete for and Allocate Resources During Financial and Enrollment Fluctuations? Monetary resources in community colleges are sometimes adequate, often scarce, and rarely abundant. Resources change from year to year as enrollments and the economy fluctuate. At the same time, faculty and administrators are always looking to grow and expand programs, to innovate, and to do more. With so much of an institution's budget allocated to fixed costs, the amount of discretionary money is truly limited, and the number of new positions that can be added in any year is small. All of this suggests that the competition for institutional resources in the community college is often intense. Although colleges choose to respond to that competition in a variety of ways, it is fairly safe to assume that those who best demonstrate that their use of the resources will advance core institutional goals—student learning and student success—will have an advantage in the competition.

Student affairs practice is thus often at a disadvantage, because there are always questions about the impact and value of (at least some) student services. For example, questions about counseling—about what role it should play, its focus, and the return on investment made in it—are eternal, and as noted earlier, student activities are often characterized as "fluff." The tendency for some student affairs professionals is to become defensive and to complain that "they" just don't understand how valuable and important student services are. Unfortunately, in this environment, complaining is not enough! As one president said in response to our survey, "Increased enrollments and scarcer resources mean more expectations for student services."

To compete successfully for limited community college resources, student affairs leaders have to do several things. First, they must determine, using good data, what really matters in the work they do: what programs and services contribute significantly to student learning, development, and success. Next, they have to be willing to reallocate existing resources appropriately to the programs and services that best serve those goals. This does not necessarily mean eliminating entire programs or services, but it does mean taking a serious look at return on investment and investing more where the greatest return is likely to be. This is often difficult, if not painful, for on occasion it means letting go of or reducing programs that we truly love, because they may not be the ones that are effective. Only after taking these steps can student affairs professionals ask for additional resources and make the case that the resources will be used to fund programs and services that demonstrably work and significantly advance the institution's mission.

Conclusion

The community college student affairs profession, much like the people who populate it, struggles with essential questions of meaning and purpose: Who are we? What really matters to us? What are our values and how do they guide our behavior? In suggesting some common definitions for the profession, delineating core values, and identifying major issues, this chapter has attempted to answer those questions and has set the stage for the discussions that will follow in the rest of this volume. Those discussions will both challenge community college student affairs professionals and suggest that they have a real opportunity to "seize the moment." For although the issues facing our profession today are real, they are also manageable. Our core values still work to anchor the profession, data can be collected, analyzed, and used to drive both discussion and action, and community college student affairs professionals can embrace the work that needs to be done and show—with both anecdotes and evidence—that what they do really matters to their institutions, to their colleagues, and most importantly, to their students.

References

American College Personnel Association. "The Student Learning Imperative: Implications for Student Affairs." *Journal of College Student Development,* 1996, *37,* 118–122.

American Council on Education. "The Student Personnel Point of View." In G. T. Saddlemire and A. L. Rents (eds.), *Student Affairs: A Profession's Heritage: Significant*

Articles, Authors, Issues, and Documents. Carbondale, Ill.: American College Personnel Association, 1983.

Helfgot, S. R. "Introduction." In M. M. Culp and S. R. Helfgot (eds.), *Life at the Edge of the Wave: Lessons from the Community College.* Washington, D.C.: National Association of Student Personnel Administrators, 1998.

Helfgot, S. R., and Culp, M. M. (eds.). *Promoting Student Success in the Community College.* New Directions for Student Services, no. 69. San Francisco: Jossey-Bass, 1995.

Keyser, J. S. (ed.). *Traverse City Statement: Toward the Future Vitality of Student Development Services.* Iowa City: American College Testing Program, 1984.

League for Innovation in the Community College. "Assuring Student Success in the Community College: The Role of Student Development Professionals." Laguna Hills, Calif.: League for Innovation in the Community College, 1987.

Matson, J. E. "Student Personnel Work Four Years Later: The Carnegie Study and Its Impact." In T. O'Banion and A. Thurston (eds.), *Student Development Programs in the Community Junior College.* Englewood Cliffs, N. J.: Prentice Hall, 1972.

McClenney, K. M. "Keeping America's Promise: Challenges for Community Colleges." In K. Boswell and C. D. Wilson (eds.), *Keeping America's Promise: A Report on the Future of the Community College.* Denver: Education Commission of the States and The League for Innovation in the Community College, 2004. http://www.communitycollegepolicy.org/pdf/KeepingAmericasPromise.pdf. Accessed July 6, 2005.

National Council on Student Development. "Toward the Future Vitality of Student Development Services: Redefining the Legacy in 2004." Transcript of a colloquium at the National Council on Student Development annual conference, Orlando, Fla., Oct. 2004.

O'Banion, T. "Toward the Future Vitality of Student Development: Redefining the Legacy." Paper presented at the National Council on Student Development annual conference, Orlando, Fla., Oct. 2004.

STEVEN R. HELFGOT is vice chancellor for student development and community affairs at the Maricopa Community Colleges in Arizona.

2

Student affairs practitioners often rely on anecdotal evidence when asked to demonstrate their contributions to the community college, but their future may depend on their ability to become more data-based and outcomes-oriented. This chapter discusses the need for a culture of evidence in student affairs, describes how to build such a culture, and provides examples of effectiveness studies and program evaluation cycles.

Building a Culture of Evidence in Student Affairs

Martha Oburn

Concerns about accountability in higher education have been around for decades. In a 1986 address to the Southern Regional Education Board, Boling observed that people "want proof that the education we offer has value, quality, and effectiveness" (p. 690). In response to this and similar statements, regional accrediting agencies and state oversight boards developed processes designed to ensure that the public had the proof it demanded.

The accountability movement accelerated in the years following Boling's address, and in the 1990s many states implemented statewide assessment systems that included sets of quality indicators. Instead of focusing on traditional measures of accountability such as the number of students attending or taking courses, the new systems focused on educational outcomes. Several states even tied funding to performance, which motivated institutions to increase their funding base by defining and reaching ambitious institutional goals.

The need to demonstrate effectiveness in order to remain accredited or receive state funding changed the way community colleges look at student affairs programs and services. Prior to the emphasis on effectiveness and quality, colleges tended to focus their assessment and planning efforts on individual instructional programs. The shift toward accountability, however, forced community colleges to look at assessment, evaluation, and planning in the context of the entire institution, not just academic departments. Almost overnight, it became essential for student affairs practitioners to

The author would like to thank Marguerite M. Culp for her assistance in organizing and editing this chapter.

demonstrate that they offer high-quality services, can define and document outcomes, and contribute to the institution's overall effectiveness.

Initially, student affairs practitioners responded to requests to demonstrate their contributions to the institution by counting the number of students using a specific service or collecting anecdotal data about students whose lives were positively changed by its programs and services. These efforts, unfortunately, did not include hard data and thus were not able to prove that the programs and services offered made a difference to the institution's mission. Gradually, student affairs leaders realized that if they were to remain a central component of their institutions, they had to build strong *cultures of evidence* to demonstrate their effectiveness, and use data to shape key institutional decisions regarding student support services and student affairs programs and activities.

This chapter discusses the processes of preparing to build a culture of evidence in student affairs divisions and selecting the right tools to measure and evaluate student affairs programs and activities effectively. The chapter also describes how to use data intelligently, and how to determine if and how student affairs programs and services make a difference in the community college.

Preparing to Build a Culture of Evidence

Building a culture of evidence begins with the assertion that community colleges must not only measure the effectiveness of instructional programs but also assess the quality and contributions of support services and other cocurricular programs. In addition, building a culture of evidence involves more than just assessment. To actually implement an institutional process, community colleges must collectively define purposes and expectations, develop outcomes measures, collect and analyze data related to those measures, and use the results for the next cycle of activity (Nichols, 1991). Furthermore, building a culture of evidence requires a willingness to leverage student affairs knowledge and expertise, create partnerships with faculty and administrators, and anticipate the problems and pitfalls associated with moving from an anecdotal to a data-based culture.

Community colleges can take many approaches to creating institutional effectiveness models, but successful approaches share two characteristics. First, the college develops a philosophical approach to institutional effectiveness that moves away from an assumption of the inherent value of educational processes to one that emphasizes documentation of educational plans, actions, and outcomes. Second, the college creates systematic, ongoing, and inclusive data collection and dissemination processes that support decision making at all levels (Pacheco, 1999).

Current models of institutional effectiveness rely less on quantitative indicators that consider the number of students participating in a certain project or activity, and more on quality indicators that incorporate student learning outcomes. These outcomes focus on changes in student behaviors resulting from the interactions between students and college faculty and staff. For example, rather than merely assessing the quality of an instructional program by counting its graduates, current assessment models allow colleges to measure quality in relation to the degree to which that program's graduates demonstrate mastery of the knowledge and skill sets associated with their program of study.

An emerging trend in institutional effectiveness is the incorporation of concepts from the quality movement, originally rooted in business and industry, into higher education evaluation systems. The Malcolm Baldrige National Quality Award, for example, is a federally sponsored quality initiative that provides criteria educational institutions can use to determine the quality of their institutions (Baldrige National Quality Program, 2005). Colleges adopting this approach use Baldrige criteria and strategies to demonstrate excellence and measure quality. Incorporating these or similar criteria and strategies may be an effective way for community college student affairs practitioners to start building a culture of evidence in their institution. The following recommendations may also be helpful.

Leverage Practitioners' Knowledge and Expertise. The community college's struggle to demonstrate its effectiveness provides student affairs practitioners with unique opportunities to become more integrated into critical institutional processes and to use their understanding of and contacts with students in such a way that their contributions are seen as intrinsic to the institution's mission. To accomplish this, however, student affairs practitioners must be willing to assume additional responsibilities and connect with institutional effectiveness processes.

To begin, practitioners must understand how the college is approaching the task of demonstrating that it provides quality programs and services. This understanding can be arrived at by asking four questions: How does the college approach institutional effectiveness? Is the process well defined and established? If the processes are focused on accrediting or state mandates, what are those mandates? How is student affairs integrated into the ongoing institutional effectiveness process, including planning and budgeting?

Knowing where the institution is in its institutional effectiveness process can help student affairs practitioners develop strategies that will increase their chances of becoming valued partners in areas where they are not and maintaining their status where they are already valued. If the college has an established institutional effectiveness process, it is critical that student affairs practitioners have well-articulated assessment measures that reflect the overall direction of the institution. If the college lacks an established institutional effectiveness process, student affairs practitioners can take the lead in developing outcomes-based processes, identifying their own measures, reporting results to the college community, and helping college leaders use the results to enhance systematic decision making. Student affairs practitioners, however, must tie their measures to student outcomes.

For example, an analysis of the completion rates of various groups of students receiving financial aid is more helpful to the institution than a report outlining the number of students receiving aid and the award amounts.

When community colleges review assessment results and use them to drive new projects or implement change, student affairs practitioners must participate in or even lead the review in order to enhance their role in institutional effectiveness processes. For example, many states now ask community colleges to compare their retention and graduation rates to state or national norms and to implement strategies that increase the number of students who remain enrolled and reach their educational and career goals. If student affairs practitioners are involved in reviewing and developing responses to the data, they can use their knowledge of student development and learning theory to help colleagues understand the importance of integrating student affairs programs (for example, advising, assessment, career counseling, orientation, student activities, and support for at-risk students) into the community college's student success model, thus strengthening it and demonstrating the importance of student affairs programs to the community college's mission.

Create Partnerships with Faculty and Administrators. Collaborative relationships with representatives from key areas in the college are essential in helping student affairs practitioners develop a culture of evidence. For example, demonstrating the effectiveness of a certain program or service requires access to and analysis of data. Therefore, student affairs practitioners should develop relationships with staff members in institutional research and the information technology areas. By working with colleagues who understand data systems and support data analysis, student affairs practitioners will be able to develop their own mechanisms for reporting findings that demonstrate the impact of student affairs programs and services on the educational processes of the college. Without this collaboration, it will be difficult to develop or analyze the necessary information. In addition, student affairs practitioners must work closely with faculty to support the implementation of instructional improvement projects. By incorporating counseling, advising, or tutoring interventions into these projects, student affairs practitioners can demonstrate the direct effects of those services on improving student learning outcomes. A final necessary partnership is with the administrators who make budget decisions, both inside and outside of student affairs. Whether these decisions are made by broad-based committees, the president's cabinet, or specific individuals, student affairs leaders must cultivate relationships with these decision makers, not only during the budget cycle but throughout the year. The most effective way to build relationships with decision makers is to continually generate and share evidence that demonstrates how student affairs contributes to student learning, student success, and the institution's mission in an organized, systematic manner.

Anticipate Problems and Pitfalls. Although opportunities exist for student affairs practitioners to play a strong role in implementing or enhancing institutional effectiveness, practitioners must remember that the process often comes with its own challenges. First, it is important to realize that change rarely happens on its own; it takes focused effort on the part of student affairs staff to understand existing institutional practices and to get involved in institutional effectiveness projects. Second, inclusion in institutional effectiveness projects and practices does not happen overnight. However, if student affairs staff can take the perspective that incremental change will lead to systemic change, they will be able to develop long-range strategies that will make a difference over time. Third, it is important to realize that not everyone in student affairs divisions will support or even understand the importance of becoming involved in institutional effectiveness processes. Some will continue to assume that the intrinsic value of what they do will be recognized and appreciated—even as they complain about not being included as part of the mainstream of educational activity. To help these staff members, student affairs leaders need to offer professional development opportunities designed to expand the knowledge base and skill sets of all practitioners.

Finally, although the process of creating a culture of evidence may seem too daunting to begin, practitioners must realize that they have to start somewhere. Like the students with whom they work, student affairs practitioners cannot finish a race they choose not to enter. There may be disappointments and mistakes along the way—it is, after all, a learning process—but there will be many rewards as practitioners succeed in replacing anecdotal cultures with cultures of evidence.

Selecting the Right Tools and Demonstrating Effectiveness

Building a culture of evidence requires that practitioners develop shared definitions, ask the right questions to determine what really matters, select the tools that will allow them to find the answers, and use these tools and the resulting data effectively.

Start with Clear Definitions. Practitioners often use terms like *assessment, evaluation,* and *research* interchangeably, although each has a distinct meaning and use. Assessment focuses on gathering, analyzing, and interpreting data in order to guide practice and demonstrate program effectiveness, whereas evaluation uses assessment evidence to improve the effectiveness of a program, department, or institution (Upcraft and Schuh, 1996). Traditionally, both activities are institution-specific. Research, in contrast, "guides theory and tests concepts" (Schuh and Upcraft, 2001, p. 5), follows stringent guidelines, and frequently has an impact beyond a single institution.

Ask the Right Questions. Student affairs practitioners have a vested interest in creating a culture of evidence for student affairs, but the process must begin with a willingness to ask and honestly answer three essential questions: Are practitioners offering services that students and faculty need to enhance student learning and increase student success? Do the services offered make a difference to the institution and its mission? Can practitioners prove that their services are needed and make a difference?

Select the Most Effective Assessment Tools. In selecting and using assessment tools to answer the preceding questions, student affairs practitioners should select instruments that have the capacity to provide relevant data, use multiple data-gathering techniques to increase the ability to generate accurate pictures and useful recommendations, and always disaggregate the data (for example, analyze data by subgroups). When used intelligently, assessment tools help student affairs practitioners identify needs, document program quality, compete for and allocate resources, and document the reasons why they offer (or choose not to offer) specific programs or services.

Demonstrate Need. Resources are finite, yet student and faculty needs are infinite. Everyone agrees that institutions must recruit, admit, advise, and register students, and offer financial aid, but the form these services take once students enroll depends on the college's mission and financial health, student demographics, and the relationship between student affairs and academic affairs.

Traditionally, needs analysis surveys and focus groups are the tools of choice for identifying student and faculty needs. The first tool allows practitioners to gather data quickly from a large number of faculty and students (current, prospective, or former), compile and disaggregate the data, and evaluate results. The second tool allows practitioners to minimize the limits of a paper-and-pencil survey by interacting with participants and helping students distinguish between "wants" and "needs." In general, using both tools increases the reliability of the needs analysis data.

Tracking use of services, which involves little more than counting participants and disaggregating data by gender, ethnicity, age, enrollment status, and other demographic variables, is another strategy that institutions often use to document student participation, and by inference, students' needs for a specific service. Programs may collect data from users every day or during designated weeks throughout the term, but the keys to success are using the data to take an honest look at how effectively student affairs reaches various subpopulations in the college, and asking the right follow-up questions. Two examples demonstrate the importance of asking the right follow-up questions when analyzing use-of-services data. If data reveal that the career center serves 45 percent of the college's African American students but only·5 percent of its Asian American, Latino-Latina, and Native American students, then prior to acting on the data student affairs practitioners should ask if low usage by the three latter groups is a consequence of lack of visibility, lack of interest in the concept of career counseling, materials and services that do not meet student needs, or staffing patterns. Similarly, if 90 percent of faculty members indicate that the college needs a referral system for academically at-risk students but only 3 percent of faculty use it, then student affairs practitioners must ask the following questions before acting on the data: What is the size of the at-risk student population? Are there significant differences between faculty members who use the referral system and faculty members who do not?

Document Effectiveness. Efforts to measure program effectiveness often start with measuring satisfaction with services among the community college's many stakeholders: students, faculty, upper-division institutions, employers, community members, and K–12 representatives. Once again, focus groups and satisfaction surveys are the tools of choice. Satisfaction surveys may be standardized nationally or developed locally, and they may be completed each time services are used (point-of-service), once a year, or at designated times throughout the year. Survey instruments can be completed where services are delivered in the classroom, at home, on the Web, or over the telephone. The key, as always, is to gather, disaggregate, and evaluate data in a systematic manner and to use the results to modify existing programs.

Institutions cannot assume that all services that receive high user-satisfaction scores are effective, just as they cannot assume that all services that receive low scores are ineffective. The key, once again, is to ask the right follow-up questions. For example, advisers who prevent students from registering for a course if they do not have the required prerequisites often receive lower satisfaction scores than other student affairs practitioners, yet they are doing the job the community college wants them to do. Before acting on any data provided by satisfaction surveys, practitioners must ask the following questions: Are students at our institution more or less satisfied with a specific program or service than students at comparable institutions? When compared with results from previous years, are this year's students more or less satisfied with specific programs and services? How satisfied are faculty members with specific programs and services provided by the student affairs division? Has their degree of satisfaction changed over time? What feedback do colleges and universities to which our students transfer provide about the quality of student affairs programs and services at our college?

Determine Whether Services Make a Difference to Students. After selecting the right assessment tools, the second and more challenging step in demonstrating effectiveness is to determine if services make a difference to those who use them—and if that difference is consistent with the institution's mission and goals. National surveys like the Community College Survey of Student Engagement (Evelyn, 2004) that ask students to assess their educational experiences yield valuable information and allow comparisons across institutions; however, student affairs practitioners usually need to supplement these surveys with carefully constructed, institution-based assessment studies that seek answers to essential questions and measure how specific services contribute to the community college's mission. Examples of several localized assessment studies and essential questions are shown in Table 2.1.

Table 2.1. Essential Questions and Sample Assessment Studies for Selected Student Affairs Programs and Services

Service	Essential Question	Suggested Study to Answer Question
Advising	Are new students without a major more likely to leave during or after their first term or year than students who have declared a major?	Compare the retention rates of a random sample of undecided students with a random sample of students with declared majors. Control for test scores and previous educational background.
Career counseling	Does completing a career-counseling class increase the probability that undecided students will remain in college and graduate?	Compare retention and graduation rates of undecided students who complete a career-counseling class with the rates for undecided students who do not enroll or who enroll but withdraw. Control for test scores and previous educational background.
College success or First-Year Experience course	Does completing a college success or first-year experience course increase the chances a student will remain in college and graduate?	Compare retention and graduation rates of students who complete a college success or first-year experience course with the rates for students who do not enroll or who enroll but withdraw. Control for test scores and previous educational background.
Counselors in the learning community	Does involving a counselor in designing and implementing a learning community increase its effectiveness?	Compare the course completion and retention rates of students in learning communities that include a counselor with the rates for communities that do not include a counselor.
Financial aid	Are students whose financial need is met completely by the institution more likely to remain in college and graduate than those whose need is only partially met?	Compare term-by-term retention and graduation rates of financial aid recipients whose need is met with recipients who have unmet financial need. Control for test scores and previous educational background.

Math anxiety	Does including a counselor-led math anxiety component in developmental math courses increase the number of students who successfully complete the courses?	Compare completion and withdrawal rates of developmental math sections of the same course with and without the counselor-led component.
Student life/student activities	Does participation in clubs, organizations, or leadership activities increase the probability that students will remain enrolled and graduate?	Controlling for test scores, grade point average, and hours worked per week, compare retention and graduation rates of students who participate in cocurricular activities and students who do not participate.
Students from underrepresented populations	Do students from minority populations participate in programs offered by the student affairs division to the same extent as students not from minority populations?	Compare participation rates in programs and services by ethnicity, gender, and other variables important to the college.
Skills courses for students in developmental classes	Does completing a course in study skills, time management, or test taking increase the probability that students will complete developmental work, remain in college, and graduate?	Compare the completion, retention, and graduation rates of students in developmental courses who complete related skills courses or seminars with the rates for students who do not enroll in or complete related skills courses or seminars.
Support group for students on probation or readmitted after suspension	Does participating in a support group increase the probability that students in academic difficulty will remain in college and graduate?	Compare GPA, retention, and graduation rates of students readmitted after suspension who participate in a support group with the rates of students on probation or suspension who do not participate in such groups.

Source: Dr. Marguerite M. Culp, Austin Community College.

Use Outside Resources. Designing assessment studies, selecting the correct tools, and analyzing data are challenging tasks, and student affairs practitioners need support from a variety of sources. On-campus resources include social science faculty as well as staff members involved with institutional research, institutional effectiveness, or information technology. Before approaching these professionals for help, however, student affairs practitioners can take advantage of two excellent resources: *Assessment Practice in Student Affairs: An Applications Manual* (Schuh and Upcraft, 2001) and *Assessment in Student Affairs: A Guide for Practitioners* (Upcraft and Schuh, 1996). As well, assistance is available from a variety of organizations, including the American College Personnel Association, American College Testing Service, Clearinghouse for Higher Education Assessment, Educational Testing Service, National Center for Higher Education Management Systems, and the National Association of Student Personnel Administrators. (See Chapter Seven for more information about these and other assessment resources.)

Understand the Importance of Baseline Data and Pilot Tests. Before leading a focus group, administering locally developed or nationally standardized instruments, implementing new programs, or significantly changing existing programs, practitioners must gather baseline data and pilot-test programs and procedures. Baseline data (such as retention rates, completion rates, grade distributions, and satisfaction with and use of services) provide a "before" picture of the institution and allow the college to measure realistically the impact of a new program, service, or procedure. Pilot studies allow student affairs to conduct trial runs of new or modified programs, services, and instruments at the micro level, evaluate feedback and outcomes, and address weaknesses before rolling out institution-wide implementations. As many practitioners have discovered, programs and procedures that look good on paper can implode in the real world, creating image problems for student affairs leaders. Better to take a few days to pilot-test than to spend weeks, or sometimes months, doing damage control.

Steps to Using Data Intelligently

Knowing how to ask essential questions and select the most appropriate assessment tools is a good start, but it's only a start. Student affairs practitioners must analyze, evaluate, and share data generated by assessment studies, and use the resulting information in evaluating services, planning for the future, and allocating resources. The following steps can guide practitioners in using assessment data intelligently.

Step 1: Create an Annual Evaluation Schedule. Student affairs practitioners must publicize to everyone in the college community when, why, and how their programs are evaluated, where to access evaluation results, and how results will be used to improve programs and services. This can be accomplished by creating an annual evaluation schedule and sharing it with college faculty, staff, and administrators. Table 2.2 outlines the 2002–03 program evaluation schedule followed by student affairs practitioners at Austin Community College (Texas). The schedule was distributed to selected faculty and staff, all administrators, and all new faculty members, as well as posted on the college's intranet, sending a powerful message to the college community about the professionalism and culture of evidence in the student affairs division.

Step 2: Evaluate and Share Results Throughout the Academic Year. Academic and student affairs leaders must review needs analysis results at the beginning of every term to identify emerging trends and verify that the college is offering services that students and faculty need. Practitioners should review point-of-service evaluation results throughout the year in order strengthen services and reallocate resources. As they become available, data from evaluation of services, assessment studies, cost-to-benefit analyses, and benchmarking comparisons should be shared with student affairs leaders and should be given to staff members during strategic planning and budget development sessions. At the beginning of each term, the senior student affairs officer should issue a report to the institution describing new students, their needs, and the services available to meet these needs. At the end of the academic year, student affairs leaders should issue a brief report on the quality and effectiveness of their services.

Step 3: Present Results in Easy-to-Read and Informative Formats. Student affairs leaders should present assessment results in easy-to-read formats that appeal to different audiences but share the following core characteristics: an accurate description of the assessment activities and their limitations, clear conclusions, recommended changes, and next steps. College leaders benefit from reading executive summaries of each assessment activity that include budget implications, action plans, and outcome measures. Faculty and staff not associated with student affairs divisions should receive a one-page document at the end of every year that outlines major contributions of student affairs, assessment results, and proposed changes. The document should also contain a link to the Web site where data can be accessed. Student affairs practitioners must have access to all the information generated by assessment studies related to their areas, as well as executive summaries of studies related to other areas, in order to make intelligent decisions during strategic planning, budget development, and goal-setting sessions.

Conclusion

Sixty-eight percent of the presidents and student affairs leaders who responded to the survey conducted for this volume (see the Editors' Notes for a description of the survey, and the Appendix for detailed survey results) identified the demand for accountability and the need to quantify results as challenges that could threaten the future of student affairs practice or

Table 2.2. Basic Program Evaluation Cycle: Retention and Student Services, Austin Community College, 2002–03

Program	Procedure	Responsible Leader(s)/ Frequency	Results Available From/When	Results Used By/To
Admissions and records, advising and counseling services, financial aid	Point-of-service evaluation forms (written)	Director or dean to whom program reports	Director or dean to whom program reports	Staff members use results to strengthen existing services and identify and deal with problem areas.
		Six weeks during year (three peak and three nonpeak)	October, February, August	
Campus-based student services	Intake forms (computer-tabulated) to measure student needs, traffic patterns, and frequency of use of major services	Campus deans of student services	Campus deans	Campus deans and their staffs use results to strengthen existing programs and services and identify and deal with problem areas.
		Six weeks during year (three peak and three nonpeak)	Fall, spring, summer registration	
Orientation	Written evaluation from small group sessions, self-paced orientation booklet, and online orientation	Campus deans of student services	Senior student affairs officer	Deans and members of the orientation committee use results to strengthen existing orientation options, identify gaps, and recommend new strategies.
		At the completion of the orientation experience	December 1 for the previous year	

Registration	Registration review (cross-functional focus group including students, staff, faculty, and administrators)	Senior student affairs officer Within two weeks of the end of fall and spring registration	Senior student affairs officer Analysis of strengths and weaknesses available October 1	Senior student affairs officer assigns identified problems to appropriate administrators for resolution and issues a report outlining how each was resolved before the start of the next registration period.
Major programs offered by retention and student services	Student need for/satisfaction survey with student services survey: *graduate* version and *currently enrolled* version	Senior student affairs officer, associate vice president for institutional effectiveness Graduates surveyed in even years; currently enrolled students surveyed in odd years	Senior student affairs officer December 1 following the academic year in which surveys were completed	Student affairs staff members use results during operational and strategic planning sessions to strengthen, add, or eliminate programs.
Student affairs division	Faculty satisfaction with student services	Associate vice president for institutional effectiveness Annual survey distributed and tabulated by the office of institutional effectiveness	Office of institutional effectiveness Late spring each year	Student affairs staff members use results during operational and strategic planning sessions to strengthen, add, or eliminate programs and identify campus-based challenges.

Source: Dr. Marguerite M. Culp, Austin Community College.

change the way practitioners do business. Building a culture of evidence, then, clearly matters to the student affairs profession and to community colleges in general. Yet although some student affairs practitioners use sophisticated data-gathering strategies to demonstrate that they offer quality programs and contribute significantly, far too many others continue to rely on anecdotal and numerical head count data to document their effectiveness. As this chapter demonstrates, that approach is no longer acceptable. Replacing anecdotal cultures with cultures of evidence is not an easy task, but with committed student affairs leaders, partners, tools, and training, it can be done. Student affairs practitioners who rely on data to guide programming and budgeting decisions will strengthen the profession as well as their institutions by demonstrating that student affairs divisions offer quality programs that contribute significantly to student access, learning, and success.

References

Baldrige National Quality Program. "Education Criteria for Performance Excellence." Gaithersburg, Md.: Baldrige National Quality Program, 2005. http://www.quality.nist.gov/PDF_files/2005_Education_Criteria.pdf. Accessed May 4, 2005.

Boling, E. "The Public Concern for Quality in Education." Paper presented at the Southern Regional Education Board meeting, Boca Raton, Fla., June 1986.

Evelyn, J. "Community Colleges Struggle to Foster Engagement, Survey Finds." *Chronicle of Higher Education*, Dec. 3, 2004, p. A37.

Nichols, J. *A Practitioner's Handbook for Institutional Effectiveness and Student Outcomes Assessment Implementation.* Edison, N.J.: Agathon, 1991.

Pacheco, A. "Culture of Evidence." *Assessment and Accountability Forum*, 1999, 9(2). http://smccd.net/accounts/csmresearch/Assessing/Culture_of_Evidence_Pacheco.doc. Accessed May 6, 2005.

Schuh, J., and Upcraft, M. *Assessment Practice in Student Affairs: An Applications Manual.* San Francisco: Jossey-Bass, 2001.

Upcraft, M., and Schuh, J. *Assessment in Student Affairs: A Guide for Practitioners.* San Francisco: Jossey-Bass, 1996.

MARTHA OBURN is associate vice chancellor for institutional effectiveness at North Harris Montgomery Community College in Texas.

3

*Student affairs practitioners must reconceptualize
traditional support services in order to use the resources
allocated to them more effectively, meet the needs of
today's students, and increase their value to community
colleges. This chapter identifies student affairs programs
that are vital to the community college's mission,
describes best practices in community college student
affairs, and demonstrates why traditional support
services are essential to the success of the contemporary
community college.*

Increasing the Value of Traditional Support Services

Marguerite M. Culp

Traditional student support services such as advising, articulation, assessment, counseling, orientation, outreach, and student activities, as well as targeted programs for graduates, program completers, and at-risk students, have survived countless budget challenges, institutional redesigns, name changes, and reporting structures through the years. Despite these challenges, student support services have survived because practitioners focused on one organizing belief: their mission was to help students succeed. This lifelong commitment to student success places student affairs practitioners in a unique position to help community colleges respond to today's challenges and become true learning-centered institutions. To be more effective, however, practitioners must strengthen the student support services that are traditionally offered in the community college, adapt these services to meet the needs of new student populations (online learners, for example), and use technology both to increase the availability of support services and to make them more cost-effective. This chapter suggests that student affairs practitioners need to focus on creating programs that encourage individuals to pursue higher education, convert applicants into successful students by connecting them to the institution and helping them make sense of their experiences, encourage students to become self-sufficient, and assist graduates and program completers to take the next step when they reach their educational and career goals at the community college.

NEW DIRECTIONS FOR COMMUNITY COLLEGES, no. 131, Fall 2005   © Wiley Periodicals, Inc.

Keeping the Promise of the Open Door

Viewed by many as "colleges of opportunity for the underprepared and the underrepresented, those new to the country and new to higher education, those needing a second chance and those needing a new start" (Helfgot and Culp, 1995, p. 1), community colleges have altered the landscape of American higher education. But some potential students, especially those from low-income or minority families, do not know how to negotiate the higher education bureaucracy (Evelyn, 2004). These students do not understand how to apply to or finance college, are often academically underprepared, view testing with terror, lack support systems, or believe that college is not for them. These are the students that student affairs practitioners must identify and serve if community colleges are to keep the promise of the open door alive. To accomplish this, student affairs leaders must connect with their colleagues in the K–12 system and create partnerships with business and civic groups.

Connect with the K–12 System. Community college educators have a vested interest in helping elementary, middle, and secondary school students understand the link between education and success, the need to complete high school, and the importance of developing strong math, science, and communication skills. Community college educators also have a vested interest in helping K–12 leaders understand the important role community colleges can play in improving high school completion rates, augmenting student support services at all levels, and assisting guidance counselors, teachers, and parents in understanding the community college's role in higher education and the community.

At Austin Community College (ACC) in Texas, as in many institutions across the country, academic and student affairs personnel collaborate to conduct summer camps for middle school students from at-risk populations, primarily those from low socioeconomic areas whose parents never attended college. During the academic year, ACC students serve as tutors and mentors to elementary and middle school students in schools with low graduation and college-attendance rates. ACC counselors and advisers are assigned to high schools in the college's service area, are on-site at specific times to assist students and faculty, and are available via telephone and e-mail throughout the year. Student affairs staff also conduct test preparation and career choice sessions for high school students and GED candidates, as well as workshops to help parents understand the importance of education beyond high school, the college admissions process, how to finance the costs of college, and their role in encouraging family members to enter and succeed in college (Culp, 2001).

Connections between the K–12 system and community colleges can also take place through strategic initiatives and decisions at the high school level. For example, in 2003 San Marcos High School in central Texas took a bold step toward connecting graduates with the local community college by requiring all seniors who had not applied to college to complete an Austin Community College application. Student affairs practitioners followed up with workshops for parents and prospective students, many of whom later enrolled at the college (Matthews, 2004).

In another example, the Community College of Baltimore County (CCBC) in Maryland partners with twenty-five Baltimore County public high schools to help students develop college-readiness skills. Coordinated by the dean of learning and student development at CCBC's Essex campus, program staff administer Accuplacer, the College Board's placement system, to high school sophomores and juniors during a half-day visit to a CCBC campus, which also includes information about the college, a tour, and lunch. High school counselors use Accuplacer results to determine if a student is college-ready, on track for readiness, or in need of additional assistance. CCBC works with high schools to improve curriculum alignment (middle, high school, and community college faculty work in vertical teams to examine specific academic areas), offers dual enrollment (allows high school students to enroll in college classes), provides precollege institutes to students (free-credit and noncredit workshops and courses), organizes career days (campus events that include motivational speakers, interpretation of instruments designed to help students identify their career interests, and interaction with faculty and local employers), and offers professional development activities for middle and high school teachers. During a three-year period, one high school participating in CCBC's program increased the number of graduates enrolling in college from 39 to 58 percent and raised its students' mean SAT scores from 890 to 1035 (Peterka, 2003).

Partner with Business and Community Groups. There are not enough student affairs practitioners to visit every high school, business, government agency, civic group, religious organization, or home in a community college's service area, but there are enough to recruit community members to serve as champions, mentors, and advocates of the community college's programs. Community-based advisory boards and alumni help hundreds of student affairs programs across the country assess community needs, identify gaps, evaluate services, and lobby for resources. Partnerships with existing networks such as churches, service organizations, and tribal groups serving large African-American, Hispanic, or Native American populations can help provide access, information, and support to prospective students and their families. Austin Community College, for example, is partnering with Saint Edward's University, the Austin Independent School District, the Austin Latino Alliance, and Austin Interfaith to create ENLACE (Engaging Latino Communities for Education), a program designed to produce more Latino high school and college graduates in Austin (Intercultural Development Research Association, 2001).

Partnerships with business, civic, and charitable groups can also lead to scholarships, jobs, internships, and mentoring programs for students and can help encourage them to finish high school and continue their education in the community college. The Bill and Melinda Gates Foundation recently awarded $6 million to LaGuardia Community College (New York) to create ten new early college high schools on college campuses and $5.4 million to Portland Community College (Oregon) to expand its Gateway to College Program for students who have dropped out of high school (LaRose, 2005). In 1999, with help from the Department of Education and generous community members, Genesee Community College (New York) created a fund, now totaling more than $500,000, to provide emergency financial assistance to at-risk students (Burcham, 2005a).

Using Assessment and Placement to Transform Applicants into Successful Students

Although community colleges enroll a significant number of students, data indicate that "eighteen- to twenty-two-year-olds . . . drop out . . . at much higher rates than would be expected from their abilities, aspirations, and family backgrounds" (Astin, 1993, p. 417) and "nearly half of all beginning students leave . . . before the start of their second year" (Tinto, 1996, p. 101). Students cannot succeed unless institutions know who they are, what they know, what they need, where they want to go, and where they are in their educational process. The most effective way to acquire this information is through an institution-wide commitment to entry, exit, and classroom assessment (League for Innovation in the Community College, 2004). Because no one knows students—how they think, what they need, how they learn, what alienates them, what energizes them—as well as student affairs practitioners, these practitioners are well suited to collaborate with faculty to design these assessment and placement models (Kuh and Banta, 2000), although this collaboration will be most effective with direction and support from top administrators. The following steps will help student affairs practitioners design and implement assessment and placement models that can help transform community college applicants into successful students.

Step 1: Identify Competencies Needed to Enter and Exit Courses. Accurate, entry-level placement starts by helping faculty realistically define the skills students need to enter and exit every course or program of study. Student affairs staff can help faculty gather and analyze data needed to make these decisions, develop models to test alternatives and examine the consequences associated with each model, and establish realistic entry and exit competencies.

Step 2: Select Appropriate Assessment Tools. Relying on their knowledge of assessment and student development, student affairs staff can collaborate with faculty in creating models that use a variety of institutional and classroom techniques to gather information about the classes in which students should start, the support services they will need, their performance in a specific class, their progress toward educational and career goals, their satisfaction with instruction and services, and their readiness to graduate, transfer, or enter the job market. Student affairs staff can assist faculty in sorting through the strengths and weaknesses of standardized placement tests, needs analyses, and satisfaction surveys in order to select or design instruments that best meet their needs. They also can help faculty obtain immediate feedback on what students are learning in a specific class by analyzing classroom assessment and classroom research as described by Cross (1997) and suggesting interventions to improve student learning before the end of the term.

Step 3: Help Students Survive the Assessment Process. Assessment is stressful, but student affairs practitioners can design programs to reduce stress and allow students to demonstrate what they can do. Optional workshops in test preparation, anxiety management, and stress reduction help some students, and many more benefit when well-trained student affairs staff members create a welcoming atmosphere, explain the purpose of the assessment process, describe how results are used, discuss how the college uses assessment results in addition to the applicant's previous educational background to help students select their first-term classes, and outline the procedures faculty members will follow during the first week of classes to verify that students are in classes that match their skills.

Step 4: Validate Student Placement. Although entry-level assessment goes a long way toward helping students succeed, placement tests are only the first step in an effective placement model. Student affairs staff can help institutions factor high school and college preparation, work and life experiences, and years out of school into the placement equation, and they can work with faculty to validate student placement during the first week of classes. Validation is a safety net for students and a tool that allows faculty to identify students whose in-class performance is inconsistent with their initial placement based on entry-level assessment results.

Step 5: Develop Student Support Service Plans. Student affairs practitioners must use results from placement tests, needs analyses, and student self-assessments to identify the support services each student needs, to help students design a support service plan that guides course selection, and to encourage students to follow the plan. Student affairs staff members also can make a difference simply by showing an interest in students and reinforcing their need to use support services.

Step 6: Share Information in User-Friendly Formats. It is important to share assessment data with faculty and administrators across campus, but these reports should be user-friendly and easy to read. Reports crammed with unorganized information sit on shelves in community colleges across the country because faculty and staff have neither the desire nor the energy to spend weeks mining them for data. Student affairs staff must collaborate with institutional research and institutional technology teams, faculty and administrators, and students to create user-friendly reports that are specifically targeted to the needs of each group. For example, students and their advisers need to know what courses and support services the college recommends, how the college developed these recommendations, the next step if the recommendations seem valid, and the circumstances under which students can appeal their initial placement. Administrators and faculty leaders want big-picture information such as trend data with subgroup analysis by major or program, ethnicity, gender, or age. Individual faculty members want to know each student's skill level, whether their students have completed prerequisite courses, and the support services each student needs to succeed. Practitioners responsible for support services need the names and addresses (e-mail and regular mail) of students whose support service plans include their areas.

Step 7: Evaluate and Improve the Placement Model. Course placement and subsequent data analysis are always a work in progress. A cross-functional team, including representatives from student affairs, must regularly review the placement model and pay special attention to the match between the model and course grades, completion, retention rates for first-year students, and input from program areas. Faculty in academic and career programs must continuously monitor the effectiveness of the placement model as it pertains to their class completion rates, grade distributions, students' performance in higher-level courses, and retention and graduation rates.

Paying Attention to At-Risk Students

Although many community college faculty believe that all their students are at risk, it is not always practical to assess and track every student who comes in the door. Therefore, student affairs practitioners must help faculty identify and intervene with students who are known to be most at risk: those who require two or more developmental courses, have not declared a major, believe they will fail, enroll in online courses without the skills or the motivation to succeed, are on probation, or face suspension or dismissal.

Locating new at-risk students in the community college can be as simple as asking high school counselors to identify students who plan to enter the community college and will need additional help to succeed. Manchester Community College (MCC) in Connecticut uses this approach to identify low-income, first-generation students who need support to succeed in college (Sheils, 2003). MCC enrolls these students in a free Summer Training and Academic Retention Services (STARS) program, a collaborative effort between academic and student affairs divisions that includes a three-credit student development course, a one-credit study skills course, and individual sessions with mentors, tutors, and counselors. Another way to identify at-risk students is by asking students to respond to a series of questions that can reveal their chances of succeeding in the community college. Sinclair Community College (Ohio) uses this approach and asks new students to complete an online survey, calculates each student's dropout risk, and then connects those most at risk to appropriate support services (Moore and Little, 2004).

Students who require extensive developmental work before enrolling in credit-bearing classes make up another easy-to-identify at-risk group. Student affairs practitioners need to help their institutions identify and understand the needs of these students and build systems that support success (for example, by eliminating late registration, implementing mandatory assessment and placement, and limiting the number of classes developmental students can take). Practitioners also need to help institutions understand that interventions only work when developmental programs are adequately funded, supported by the institution's mission statement, and taught by qualified instructors. The Community College of Denver (Colorado) uses the College Board's Accuplacer computerized placement test in addition to a local study-skills instrument, requires mandatory placement into basic skills classes (if needed), provides numerous support services for students in developmental courses (such as supplemental learning, mentoring, and counseling), and uses a case management approach to help first-time students (Roueche, Ely, and Roueche, 2001). Austin Community College requires students who need two or more developmental courses to create educational and support service plans, register for a course designed to help them succeed in college (Transition to College Success) during their first twelve credit hours at the institution, and work with counselors to monitor their progress (Culp, 2001). At Pensacola Junior College (Florida), faculty, staff, students, and administrators offer precollegiate orientation sessions to help students requiring remediation understand how to balance school with other obligations and use college resources effectively (Elledge, 2004).

Students who are on probation or who face suspension or dismissal are another type of at-risk student whom community colleges should track, monitor, and mentor. In most cases, this means assigning each student to a student affairs practitioner who can help that student develop a personalized educational and support service plan, monitor compliance with the plan, and track academic progress. Because students on suspension or readmission after dismissal do not always make wise educational choices, community colleges must allow these students to register and attend classes only if they follow their educational and support service plans.

Students who enroll in online courses without the skills or the motivation to succeed are a unique group of at-risk students. Cerro Coso Community College (California) responded to the high attrition rate for these students by creating online support services that include assessment, orientation, an educational plan, and an online session with a counselor. The assessment component includes two self-tests that allow students to measure their technical and academic skills and determine if online learning is the best educational choice for them (Darnell and Rosenthal, 2001).

Several community colleges are pioneering approaches to identifying, tracking, and intervening with at-risk students that, if they succeed, will set the standard for every community college in the country. One of these institutions is Sinclair Community College in Ohio. Sinclair's current assessment and placement system includes an online survey to calculate the dropout risk for each student, a risk assessment for students identified as dropout risks, and the assignment of students most at risk to counselors. Sinclair's system also includes a "Student Success Plan" that is entered into the Web-based tracking system, a to-do list for each at-risk student, and a place on the Web where counselors can monitor student progress, record notes, and track completed tasks (Moore and Little, 2004).

Identifying and Managing Transition Points

Not all applicants who are admitted to a community college register, while some register but never attend classes. Many students drop out, usually during their first year or prior to the start of their second year (Tinto, 1993). Student affairs practitioners must help institutions manage the transition points when students are most likely to drop out. Postcards, automated call-out systems, and call centers (either campus-based or outsourced) are strategies that community colleges can use to encourage applicants to complete the enrollment process, help currently enrolled students register for the next term, and invite students who have dropped out to return to college. The Enrollment Management Center at Valencia Community College (Florida), for example, calls all first-time students to "check on their experiences with the college and offer suggestions for assistance" (Romano, 2004). The center also calls students after they complete fifteen to eighteen credit hours and again after they finish thirty to thirty-three credit hours in order to check on their progress and remind them of the resources available at Valencia to help them succeed (http://valenciacc.edu/lifemap/stages_pd_ps.asp).

In addition, partnerships between faculty and student affairs practitioners are essential in encouraging students to remain enrolled and reach their educational goals. Building learning-centered communities, connecting with students throughout the term, reminding students to register for the next term, and showing an interest in each student's future plans are simple strategies that pay great dividends for the students and the community college.

Helping Students Make Sense of the Institution and Their Experiences

Nationally, 30 percent of community college students are members of a minority group, more than 80 percent work full- or part-time, and many have family responsibilities (American Association of Community Colleges, 2004). In addition, 55 percent of low-income students who pursue higher education enroll in a community college (Burcham, 2005b). Research indicates that engaging these students can help them succeed in the community college (McClenney, 2004), and student affairs practitioners have significant roles to play in helping community colleges create supportive campus climates that assist students to understand, connect with, and become part of the college community. Much of this work is accomplished through orientation services, advising and counseling programs, and student life activities.

Deliver an Orientation Experience That Matters. Community college applicants are busy people who want to apply, register, pay, and start classes. Most view orientation as another hurdle, which is unfortunate, because, when done well, orientation offers new students a unique opportunity to connect with the institution, other students, and themselves. Therefore, student affairs practitioners must help faculty and staff remember what it feels like to begin college, to anticipate and answer the questions students have but do not ask, and to act as guides, interpreters, and problem-solvers for new students. Practitioners also must help everyone understand that technology can—and often does—play an important role in orienting students, but it must be used to benefit students, not just to save time and reduce personnel costs.

One way to deliver an orientation experience that matters is to incorporate orientation into every class. Student affairs leaders should encourage faculty to include information on support services in their syllabus, set aside time early in the term to talk about time management, and teach students how to study for their courses, prepare for tests, create study groups, identify what they do not know, and use support services. Student affairs practitioners can create videos, DVDs, and handouts to support their faculty colleagues, but it is important that instructors themselves demonstrate willingness not only to help students master a subject but also to help them learn how to learn.

Orientation approaches similar to the First Semester Experience at Moraine Valley Community College (MVCC) in Illinois are growing in popularity because they address the unique needs of community college students. A collaborative effort between academic and student affairs, the First Semester Experience at MVCC offers students a chance to develop study and time management skills, gain some insights into themselves and the role that education can play in their future, learn how to access services, participate in a ready-made support group, and develop an individualized master academic plan (Wright, 2003). A popular option for today's busy students is an online orientation similar to that available at Tennessee's North East State Technical Community College (Starling and Johnson, 2004) and the North Harris Montgomery Community College District in Texas (Bilides and Rockefeller, 2004). Both programs introduce students to the college's expectations and culture, available support services, and the skills needed to succeed there.

It also is important to involve families in the orientation process. Many community college students are the first in their families to attend college, and their families either do not know what to expect or view college as an extension of high school. Student affairs practitioners can involve other areas of the college in coordinating orientation opportunities for parents, spouses, siblings, and significant others to help create a better understanding of the institution's expectations, availability of support services, role of faculty members, and type of family support that will help students succeed.

Strengthen the Advising Process. After instruction, advising is the most important function of a community college, and student affairs practitioners must take the lead in helping colleges understand that advising helps students connect with the institution and make smart life and educational choices (O'Banion, 1994). Practitioners also must work with institutions to use technology to provide repetitive information about degree and program requirements, thus freeing faculty, counselors, and advisers to focus on the developmental aspects of advising (Cross, 2000).

FACTS.org, Florida's official online student advising system, is an example of how technology can be used to provide repetitive information. At this site, high school students can determine career objectives, evaluate their progress in high school, explore higher education opportunities in Florida, apply to colleges online, and choose a major. College students may access their college transcripts and grades, track progress toward college graduation, run degree audits, compare data from their transcripts against program requirements at any Florida institution, and access links to college catalogues (Graunke, 2004). By creating one data source for high schools, community colleges, and colleges and universities, Florida provides consistent information to all parties (students, parents, faculty members, and staff), encourages students to take responsibility for acquiring basic information, and allows those who advise to focus on helping students process information, explore alternatives, evaluate consequences, and make informed decisions.

Although a state system like FACTS.org is impressive, it is only one step toward creating an advising system that works. Student affairs practitioners must help community colleges use state systems effectively, understand that the information in the system is useless if it is not current, and design advising models that meet the needs of new students, returning students with or without declared majors, students on academic probation or suspension, and reentering students who have been away from college for an extended period of time.

Valencia Community College is one institution that recognizes the different advising needs of its students and successfully incorporates a state information system (FACTS.org) into its advising model. At Valencia, practitioners use LifeMap, a guide that "links all the components of Valencia (faculty, staff, courses, technology, programs, services) into a personal itinerary" to help students succeed (http://valenciacc.edu/lifemap/). Based on Valencia's developmental advising model, LifeMap outlines programs and services and defines success indicators for high school students considering college, entering students, transfer students, currently enrolled students, and students preparing to graduate. The student handbook (http://valenciacc.

edu/pdf/studenthandbook.pdf) provides an overview of LifeMap and offers tools that students can use to define their life and career goals, develop educational plans, build class schedules, and evaluate their academic success skills. New degree-seeking students also learn about LifeMap during mandatory orientation sessions. Valencia also created My Educational Plan, a software program that allows students to plan their education to meet all graduation requirements and save their plan online; My Career Plan, an online career-planning program that guides students through self-assessments and allows them to store their results as well as career and major choices; and My Portfolio, an online tool in which students can save examples of their academic work and post a résumé (Romano, 2004).

An effective advising program requires providing ongoing professional development for all who advise students. Student affairs practitioners at Monroe Community College (New York) offer the Academic Advising Atlas, a variety of workshops and online resources that support the advising process (http://www.monroecc.edu/depts/counsel/aaa/advwksp.htm). One resource, called Enriching Advisement: The Workshop Series, offers over thirty-five workshops taught by counselors, advisers, and administrators. Workshops at the 100 level introduce essential advising information, workshops at the 200 level explore advising models and the relationship of human development theory to the advising process, and workshops at the 300 level examine advanced topics such as cross-cultural advising. Monroe Community College also provides advisers with information about their advising responsibilities, connects them with local and national advising resources, and encourages them to register for workshops and online training opportunities (http://www.monroecc.edu/depts/counsel/aaa/FORFAC.htm).

Because honest feedback strengthens the advising process, student affairs practitioners must help their institutions complete evaluations of advising and individual advisers by asking students, faculty, graduates, universities, and employers to periodically rate the college's advising system. It is important, however, to look beyond satisfaction with services. How students view the community college's advising program after they graduate, as well as the number of credits lost during the transfer process, often provide valuable information about the effectiveness of a community college's advising model.

The final step in creating a quality advising model is to listen and act on what advisers observe to be emerging trends (such as declining demand for an area of study), registration problems (not enough sections offered in a subject), and student course creativity (for example, patching together courses from different programs to create their own areas of concentration). When advisers at Austin Community College noticed that many students classified as noncompleters were designing and completing their own programs of study based on employer needs rather than the college catalogue, the college created a series of Marketable Skills Awards based on course clusters identified by departments, thereby creating sensible options for students and more useful outcomes data for the institution (Culp, 2001).

Refocus and Strengthen Counseling Services. Faculty, staff, and administrators are often confused about the function and scope of counseling services in the community college. Some see counselors as highly compensated information-givers; others view counselors as pseudotherapists who have no place at a community college. In reality, community college counselors play three major roles: information giving (helping students deal with cognitive problems by obtaining and processing data), advising (assisting emotionally healthy students to deal with problems that have both emotional and cognitive content), and counseling (helping students deal with intrapersonal or interpersonal problems that are reality-based, have the potential to reduce significantly their ability to function in the community college, and may have serious consequences if left unattended). Community college counselors are not psychotherapists, a fact recognized by a growing number of institutions that contract with outside agencies to provide services for students who require more than three personal counseling sessions. Seminole Community College (Florida), for example, uses student activity fees to pay for the first three sessions; students are responsible for additional sessions, but the fee structure is based on their ability to pay (Helfgot and Culp, 2005).

As Terry O'Banion (2004), president emeritus of the League for Innovation in the Community College, noted, there will never be enough money to fund an adequate number of counseling positions, and counselors need to get over the lack of money and move on. One way to make counseling services more cost-effective is to move away from individual counseling, except in those situations where it is absolutely necessary. Counselors must reconceptualize their roles to focus on career counseling, teaching credit classes (for example, career planning, college success, and orientation), offering noncredit workshops and seminars (such as college survival skills, dealing with math anxiety, stress management, study skills, and time management), working with students in groups, collaborating with faculty to provide basic advising and counseling services, training students as counselor aides, and using their talents to design and evaluate programs and train and supervise staff.

Counselors need to forge strong relationships with their faculty colleagues. One way to do this is to help faculty deal with classroom management issues such as disruptive or unmotivated students. Another strategy is to help faculty members identify and work with students who are underperforming because they are unable to cope with personal issues such as career changes, divorce, interpersonal conflicts, and job challenges. Counselors can facilitate workshops based on selected papers by K. Patricia Cross that can help faculty explore how students learn (Cross, 1999), the relationship between cultural differences and learning preferences (Cross, 1998), strategies to develop self-motivated students (Cross, 2001), and techniques for promoting active learning (Cross, 2003). In addition, short seminars or counselor-designed Web sites can help faculty anticipate and avoid problems, know when and how to refer students to counselors, and understand students' rights and responsibilities. Finally, counselors must be able to help faculty assess student problems, schedule interventions, connect with community agencies, facilitate ongoing workshops to which faculty can refer students who need help, and provide faculty with timely and appropriate feedback.

Although community colleges are not in the business of providing long-term mental health care to students, they must respond in some way to students whose emotional problems interfere with their ability to learn, because these students have the potential to create great problems in the classroom and on the campus. Counselors can assist community colleges in avoiding or managing potential problems by creating partnerships with external agencies to provide consulting support to the college and psychological services to its students, helping faculty understand that some students who appear "disturbed" have a right to be on campus and in class, and helping faculty create classroom environments that support students with psychological disabilities. Another significant role for counselors is in helping their faculty colleagues differentiate between student behavior that is appropriate for a specific developmental stage and behavior that warrants further study, and in conducting preliminary intake interviews to identify students in need of psychological evaluations. Counselors must also help community college administrators understand the importance of establishing a budget to pay for psychological evaluations for students when the college mandates such testing but students cannot afford the costs, developing a crisis intervention model that guides responses to serious psychological challenges (suicide threats, for example), and training a crisis intervention team to implement the model.

Offer Student Life Activities That Connect Students to the College and the Community. The final step community colleges must take in helping students integrate into and make sense of their community college experiences is to offer well-developed student life programs that link students to the institution and the community, and help them make sense of their classroom experiences. This presents a significant challenge to student affairs practitioners because many community college students have work and family obligations that prevent their participation in events outside the classroom (Tinto, 1996).

One way to meet this challenge is to collaborate with faculty to connect student activities to the classroom and the curriculum. Service learning offers many opportunities for professionals in academic affairs and student affairs to work together to blend classroom knowledge with community experience. Lansing Community College (Michigan), Pima Community College (Arizona), and Trident Technical College (South Carolina) are examples of community colleges that offer introductory leadership courses and interdisciplinary service-learning opportunities for students (Byrd, 2004). Factoring participation in cocurricular activities or college-sponsored volunteer opportunities into course grades is another way for faculty members to connect the classroom to the real world, but this only happens when student affairs practitioners and faculty members work together to identify cocurricular activities that complement the classroom.

Other approaches include linking funding for clubs and organizations to community service and rewarding participation in cocurricular activities. At Prince George's Community College (Maryland), student organizations cannot qualify for institutional funds unless they include community service in their budget proposal (Dukes, 2005). Valencia Community College encourages students to participate in Dimensions of Leadership, a sequence of courses for students who want to become involved in campus life, develop their leadership skills, and earn credits toward a leadership certificate (Romano, 2004). Monroe Community College recently developed a cocurricular transcript that certifies a student's acquisition of leadership, communication, and management skills. Created by students and their advisers, the transcript is available online and can be attached to the student's official college-credit transcript (Salvador, 2004).

Student life programs are more important than ever to community colleges struggling to engage students. Student affairs practitioners need to help their faculty colleagues understand this, and must collaborate with faculty to design programs that send a clear message to students: you are part of a serious learning community that expects you to connect, reflect, and change as a result of your learning experiences—and these learning experiences do not end when you walk out of the classroom.

Helping Students Open the Next Door

The community college's job is not finished when students graduate; in fact, how the institution helps students handle this transition influences their perception of their college experience. Student affairs practitioners must offer students entering the workforce assistance with their job search, résumé writing, and interviewing techniques, and should connect these students with print, electronic, and human resources. To benefit students planning to transfer to a university, student affairs practitioners must work collaboratively with staff at four-year institutions to design shared advising programs and make sure transfer students are prepared for university life. Practitioners should also create targeted orientation sessions and support services for transfer students, and implement follow-up strategies to identify the strengths and weaknesses of the transfer process. In some community colleges, student affairs practitioners deliver these services; in others, they train the staff members who deliver the services. Whatever approach community colleges choose to take, the critical variable is involving student affairs staff in designing, implementing, and evaluating strategies that help graduates and program completers take the next step.

The Moo-vin On Program designed by the office of retention and student services at Austin Community College and the office of retention services at the University of Texas (UT) is an example of a successful collaboration that helps community college students manage the transition from a two-year institution to a major research university. In Moo-vin On, UT representatives offer small group sessions at ACC to introduce students to the transfer process, review admissions requirements, and assist with the financial aid application process. UT representatives are available at advertised times on various ACC campuses, host orientation sessions specifically for community college transfers, and conduct information sessions for ACC advisers, counselors, and faculty representatives to make sure that advising information is current and everyone is aware of future changes and trends. In addition, UT and ACC staff members maintain a listserv that allows counselors and advisers from both institutions to post questions and exchange information (Culp, 2001).

Conclusion

Traditional support services are essential to today's community college, but there are not enough resources to allow student affairs practitioners to be all things to all people. Practitioners must choose which programs and services to offer, and they must choose wisely. To do so, practitioners must understand the mission of the community college in which they work, evaluate the extent to which specific student affairs programs make a difference to this mission, determine cost-to-benefit ratios (Is there a less expensive but equally effective version of this program?), and look objectively at the opportunity costs associated with each program (By allocating resources to this program, what other programs are we unable to offer?). Student affairs practitioners also must partner with their faculty colleagues to help community colleges refine their mission, strengthen the K–12 pipeline, forge alliances with business and civic groups, give all students who enter the college a good start, provide at-risk students with additional support, and create an environment in which all students have opportunities to reach their educational and career goals. In the process, some practitioners may need to transform how they work, strengthen their current skill set, or acquire new skills. This may require institutions to provide professional development opportunities for student affairs staff members similar to those offered at the Maricopa Community Colleges (Kushibab, 2005), Austin Community College (Culp, 2001), and other institutions across the country. The cost of funding professional development opportunities for student affairs practitioners will be offset by the additional revenue generated when student retention and graduation rates increase as a result of programs provided by well-prepared and highly skilled student affairs practitioners.

References

American Association of Community Colleges. "Student Enrollment and Characteristics," 2004. http://www.aacc.nche.edu/Content/NavigationMenu/ AboutCommunity Colleges/Trends_and_Statistics/EnrollmentInfo/EnrollmentInfo.htm. Accessed May 9, 2005.

Astin, A. *What Matters in College?* San Francisco: Jossey-Bass, 1993.

Bilides, L., and Rockefeller, D. "Online Student Services." Paper presented at the National Council on Student Development annual conference, Orlando, Fla., Oct. 2004.

Burcham, J. "College Establishes Emergency Fund to Assist At-Risk Students." *Community College Times,* Jan. 18, 2005a, p. 9.

Burcham, J. "Attendance of Traditional-Age Students Up 10 Percent." *Community College Times,* Mar. 29, 2005b, p. 1.

Byrd, M. "The Imperative to Integrate Effective Service-Learning Initiatives." Paper presented at the National Council on Student Development annual conference, Orlando, Fla., Oct. 2004.

Cross, K. P. *Developing Professional Fitness Through Classroom Assessment and Classroom Research.* Mission Viejo, Calif.: League for Innovation in the Community College, 1997.

Cross, K. P. *Opening Windows on Learning.* Mission Viejo, Calif.: League for Innovation in the Community College, 1998.

Cross, K. P. *Learning Is About Making Connections.* Mission Viejo, Calif.: League for Innovation in the Community College, 1999.

Cross, K. P. "Cyber-Counseling, Virtual Registration, and Student Self-Service: Student Services in the Information Age." In M. Milliron and C. Miles (eds.), *Taking a Big Picture Look: Technology, Learning, & the Community College.* Mission Viejo, Calif.: League for Innovation in the Community College, 2000.

Cross, K. P. *Motivation: Er . . . Will That Be on the Test?* Mission Viejo, Calif.: League for Innovation in the Community College, 2001.

Cross, K. P. *Techniques for Promoting Active Learning.* Phoenix, Ariz.: League for Innovation in the Community College, 2003.

Culp, M. M. "Managing Change Without Destroying Staff, Students or Student Affairs." Paper presented at the American College Personnel Association convention, Boston, Mar. 2001.

Darnell, D., and Rosenthal, D. "Evolution of a Virtual Campus." *Community College Journal,* 2001, 71(3), 21–23.

Dukes, C. "The Hottest Issues in Student Affairs." Paper presented at the National Association of Student Personnel Administrators convention, Tampa, Fla., Mar. 2005.

Elledge, E. "Precollegiate Orientation: Personalizing the College Experience." Paper presented at the National Council on Student Development annual conference, Orlando, Fla., Oct. 2004.

Evelyn, J. "Community Colleges at a Crossroads." *Chronicle of Higher Education,* Apr. 30, 2004, p. A27.

Graunke, C. "Supporting Student Success with the Power of Online Technology." Paper presented at the National Council on Student Development annual conference, Orlando, Fla., Oct. 2004.

Helfgot, S. R., and Culp, M. M. (eds.). *Promoting Student Success in the Community College.* San Francisco: Jossey-Bass, 1995.

Helfgot, S. R., and Culp, M. M. "Student Affairs in the Community College: What Really Matters?" Paper presented at the National Association of Student Personnel Administrators convention, Tampa, Fla., Mar. 2005.

Intercultural Development Research Association. "ENLACE: Engaging Latino Communities for Education," 2001. http://www.idra.org/enlace/austin.htm. Accessed May 9, 2005.

Kuh, G. D., and Banta, T. W. "Faculty-Student Affairs Collaboration on Assessment." *About Campus*, 2000, 4(6), 4–8.

Kushibab, D. "Community College Student Services Institute." Paper presented at the National Association of Student Personnel Administrators convention, Tampa, Fla., Mar. 2005.

LaRose, M. "Early College High Schools Receive $30 Million in Grants." *Community College Times*, Jan. 4, 2005, p. 1.

League for Innovation in the Community College. "An Assessment Framework for the Community College: Measuring Student Learning and Achievement as a Means of Demonstrating Institutional Effectiveness," 2004. http://www.league.org/publication/whitepapers/files/0804.pdf. Accessed May 9, 2005.

Matthews, J. "Program Nudges Students to Go to College." *Washington Post*, May 24, 2004, p. A09.

McClenney, K. M. "Keeping America's Promise: Challenges for Community Colleges." In K. Boswell and C. D. Wilson (eds.), *Keeping America's Promise: A Report on the Future of the Community College*. Denver: Education Commission of the States and the League for Innovation in the Community College, 2004. http://www.community collegepolicy.org/pdf/KeepingAmericasPromise.pdf. Accessed July 6, 2005.

Moore, K., and Little, R. "Using Technology to Expand and Improve Student Learning." Paper presented at the League for Innovation in the Community College Vanguard Conference, Toronto, Canada, 2004.

O'Banion, T. "An Academic Advising Model." *NACADA Journal*, 1994, 14(2), 10–16.

O'Banion, T. "Toward the Future Vitality of Student Development: Redefining the Legacy." Paper presented at the National Council on Student Development annual conference, Orlando, Fla., Oct. 2004.

Peterka, C. J. "High School College Readiness: A Case Study." *NASPA Net Results*, Nov. 18, 2003, p. 3.

Romano, J. "LifeMap: A Learning-Centered System for Student Success." Paper presented at the National Council on Student Development annual conference, Orlando, Fla., Oct. 2004.

Roueche, J., Ely, E., and Roueche, S. *In Pursuit of Excellence: The Community College of Denver*. Washington, D.C.: Community College Press, 2001.

Salvador, S. "Monroe Community College." In League for Innovation in the Community College (ed.), *An Assessment Framework for the Community College: Measuring Student Learning and Achievement as a Means of Demonstrating Institutional Effectiveness*, 2004. http://www.league.org/publication/whitepapers/files/0804.pdf. Accessed May 9, 2005.

Starling, J., and Johnson, D. "New Student Online Orientation, In Step with Today's Student." Paper presented at the National Council on Student Development annual conference, Orlando, Fla., Oct. 2004.

Sheils, F. "Summer Bridge Programs 101: The Glories and the Agonies," 2003. http://www.ncsdonline.org/confer/2003/shared_journey/2nd.asp. Accessed May 9, 2005.

Tinto, V. *Leaving College: Rethinking the Causes and Cures of Student Attrition*. Chicago: University of Chicago Press, 1993.

Tinto, V. "Persistence and the First-Year Experience at the Community College: Teaching New Students to Survive, Stay, and Thrive." In J. Hankin (ed.), *The Community College: Opportunity and Access for America's First-Year Students*. Columbia: University of South Carolina, 1996.

Wright, J. "The First Semester Student Experience," 2003. http://www.ncsdonline.org/confer/2003/shared_journey/1st.asp. Accessed May 9, 2005.

MARGUERITE M. CULP, formerly senior student affairs officer at Austin Community College in Texas, is now executive director of Solutions-Oriented Consulting in Florida.

4

As community colleges embrace learning-centered practices, student affairs professionals have an opportunity to recommit to building and maintaining partnerships with their academic colleagues. This chapter explores the development, nature, and culture of learning-centered partnerships between academic and student affairs professionals, identifies best practices in community colleges, and examines the role of technology in enhancing partnership opportunities.

Connecting Academic and Student Affairs to Enhance Student Learning and Success

Paul A. Dale, Tonya M. Drake

> Only when everyone on campus—particularly academic affairs and student affairs—shares the responsibility for student learning will we be able to make significant progress in improving it.
> —American Association for Higher Education, American College Personnel Association, and National Association of Student Personnel Administrators (1998, p. 1)

Since the publication of "The Student Personnel Point of View" in 1937 (American Council on Education, 1983), much has been written about the significance of collaborative partnerships between student and academic affairs colleagues as a necessary component in achieving student learning and success. Recently, several student affairs scholars have written about the attributes and characteristics of student and academic affairs partnerships (Banta and Kuh, 1998; Culp, 1998; Schroeder, 1998). These writings identify the strategies needed to develop and maintain partnerships, describe organizational models that support and enhance partnerships, and outline skill sets for effectively navigating partnerships.

Given these and similar publications, why is collaboration between academic and student affairs still a compelling and important conversation? Although contemporary authors contend that academic and student affairs have complementary roles in helping students learn, most community college educators believe that the academic affairs area is responsible for student learning, whereas the student affairs area plays a supporting, often

NEW DIRECTIONS FOR COMMUNITY COLLEGES, no. 131, Fall 2005 © Wiley Periodicals, Inc.

minor, role. In addition, budget reductions and new organizational models have eroded the role that student affairs programs once played in the learning process. However, O'Banion's (1997) call for the creation of learning-centered colleges and the emergence of innovative learning technologies have rekindled interest in the role of student affairs programs in enhancing student learning and success.

Despite the wealth of literature focused on partnerships between personnel from student affairs and academic affairs, it is clear that students still experience a gap between the two divisions. At a recent focus group held at the Maricopa Community Colleges (Arizona), students were asked to comment on those attributes of the community college that really make a difference to them in achieving success and enhancing learning. They identified the following as particularly important: enhanced communication and sharing of information between students, faculty, and student affairs staff; expansion of holistic learning opportunities such as applied learning, problem-based learning, contextual learning, or service learning; and greater integration of students' personal, career, and educational goals with the learning that is occurring in the classroom (Maricopa Community College District, 2004). This microcosm of student experiences suggests there is still room for improvement in integrating student learning experiences in and outside the classroom.

In 1999, Terry O'Banion observed: "We make the assumption that one human being, the teacher, can ensure that thirty very different human beings, in one hour a day, three days a week, for sixteen weeks, can learn enough to become enlightened citizens, productive workers, and joyful life-long learners" (p. 3). Clearly this assumption is flawed, and as this quote demonstrates, partnerships between academic and student affairs personnel are needed now more than ever to ensure that student learning occurs. As community colleges experience significant increases in the number of underprepared students, English language learners, and students for whom the community college is their only higher education option, partnerships can generate additional resources, shared responsibilities, and multidimensional programs that increase the chances students will succeed.

This chapter explores effective academic and student affairs partnerships, demonstrates that the concept of the learning-centered college may be the lever that leads to sustainable partnerships between academic and student affairs, describes strategies to enhance partnerships, and examines the impact that emerging learning technologies will have on academic and student affairs partnerships.

Student Success and the Learning Movement

Student success and student learning have emerged as "what matters most" not just for student affairs but also for the entire college community. Greater public emphasis on accountability, including quality education and measurable outcomes, forces institutions to reexamine traditional ways of doing business. Research indicates that responsibility for student learning needs to become systemic and cut across classrooms, disciplines, departments, and divisions. Ideally, the entire college should assume collective responsibility for student success (McClenney, 2004). The learning-centered college movement, which gained momentum in the 1990s, also places greater emphasis on the principles that everyone has a role to play and can contribute to enhancing student success (Flynn, 2003) and that learning occurs any way, any place, any time (O'Banion, 1999). The learning-centered college movement provides student affairs practitioners with the impetus to further "infiltrate" the classroom and become true partners with their faculty colleagues in order to ensure that learning takes place both in and outside the classroom.

To capitalize on the learning-centered movement, student affairs practitioners must help their colleges create learning-centered cultures, strengthen staff recruitment and development, use information technology to improve and expand student learning, develop and measure learning outcomes, and create or expand learning-centered programs and strategies to ensure student success (League for Innovation in the Community College, 2004). In addition, student affairs practitioners must ask themselves some fundamental questions about the real impact of their programs on learning (Dale, 2003). For example, do traditional student affairs programs fully place learning at the core of their mission? Do student affairs practitioners understand that learning involves the whole student? Do such innovative and emerging programs as First-Year Experience, support services for distance learners, high school bridge programs, and service learning use models that are interdisciplinary and collaborative or do practitioners try to fit these programs into the traditional student affairs organizational model?

Creating a Culture of Collaboration

Cross (1998), Ewell (1997), and others argue that we need to recognize all activities and events as learning opportunities. Ewell (1997) recommends a "far closer integration between curriculum and cocurriculum than is currently the case at most institutions" (p. 10). Similarly, Harvey and Knight (1996) contend that all pedagogy should focus on the total student learning experience. As well, when viewed against the backdrop of the community college's student population that includes significant numbers of first-generation students and commuters who carve a well-worn "car-to-class-to-car" path, McClenney's findings (2004) about the importance of engagement in student learning underscore the importance of collaborative programs that engage students, link them to the college and the community, and improve their chances of succeeding in college.

Currently, there is increased interest from both student and academic affairs practitioners in expanding and strengthening innovative programs such as learning communities, service learning, and First-Year Experience. These programs often emerge out of a single division, yet programmatic outcomes can be enhanced through collaboration across multiple student and academic affairs areas. Through partnerships, these innovative programs can avoid becoming "a train on its own track isolated from its fellows and from the real way the institution does business . . . [that] either fades away fast as the latest fad or . . . finds an organizational home of its own" (Ewell, 1997, p. 4).

To create successful partnerships between academic and student affairs, it is important to take a systems perspective that acknowledges that the community college is a whole, interdependent entity in which relationships are central to organizational success, and formal and informal conversation are valued and encouraged (Senge, 1994). Kezar (2003) noted that "both structural (formal organization, rules, planning processes) and cultural strategies (dialogue, common vision, staff development) are important to the process of facilitating collaboration" (p. 14). Ewell (1997) also discusses the importance of taking a systems approach and suggests that through sustained organizational learning, student affairs and academic affairs staff can relearn and transform their respective roles.

A culture of collaboration is imperative if community colleges are to create systemic and enduring change to achieve student success and retention. Creating such a culture involves altering values, purposes, underlying assumptions, beliefs, myths, and rituals (Kezar, 2003). The entire college community—from the leadership to the frontline staff—needs to understand and accept a paradigm shift that includes new behaviors, vocabulary, and organizational norms. Before student affairs professionals can become valued partners in a learning-centered college, staff members need to become familiar with research about student learning and weave this research into their daily work. *Powerful Partnerships: A Shared Responsibility for Learning* (American Association for Higher Education, American College Personnel Association, and National Association of Student Personnel Administrators, 1998) outlines ten principles of learning and collaboration, urges student and academic affairs professionals to use these principles as guides, and emphasizes that learning is about making and maintaining connections. It also states that learning is enhanced when it takes place in the context of a compelling situation and when individuals are intrinsically tied to others as social beings. New student orientation, academic advising, and recruiting activities can more fully integrate students' readiness to learn by involving faculty. To make connections with students, faculty panels and presentations at new student orientations can be designed to share examples of classroom experiences that are integrated with purposeful activities outside of the classroom, such as service learning, cooperative work experience, and student volunteerism.

Building Partnerships Between Student Affairs and Academic Affairs

Schroeder (1998) suggests that a number of events can encourage successful partnerships between academic and student affairs divisions in the community college. These "triggering events" (p. 6) must be connected to a real and compelling college need. In addition, college leaders must send clear messages that creating partnerships is not the responsibility of only one group in the college community, and that resources will be granted only to those programs that demonstrate a shared vision and measurable outcomes.

Paradise Valley Community College (Arizona) successfully applied Schroeder's approach to increase the number of students succeeding in developmental mathematics courses. The college created the Underprepared Student Initiative, a task force including both faculty and staff from academic and student affairs areas. Members of the initiative designed a semester-long student success program that, when funded by the college and incorporated into developmental math courses, significantly increased student success in developmental mathematics (Paradise Valley Community College, 2004).

In reality, community colleges can take six steps to increase opportunities for student affairs professionals to engage in meaningful partnerships and sustainable collaborative relationships with their faculty colleagues. These steps, along with best practices from institutions that have successfully implemented them, are presented here.

Step 1: Define Partnerships as a Core Value. To sustain systemic support for collaborative partnerships, it is important that student affairs professionals help their institutional leaders and faculty colleagues understand that such partnerships are a core value of the community college. The two-year Project DEEP (Documenting Effective Educational Practice) study reports that "building cross-campus collaborations to facilitate student success is essential" and identifies twenty institutions that build effective partnerships between academic and student affairs (Kinzie and Kuh, 2004, p. 2). Although mutual respect is the foundation of these partnerships, colleges must build on this foundation by identifying internal collaboration as a core value in all institutional documents. They must also emphasize and reward internal collaborations during the college's strategic planning process, celebrate accomplishments resulting from student and academic affairs partnerships at all collegewide meetings, publicize best practices in internal college publications, and encourage additional partnerships by establishing budget incentives that promote partnerships.

Step 2: Focus on Collaboration in Professional Development Programs. Community colleges must develop a continuous professional development program that helps student affairs professionals understand the need for and acquire the skills to create effective partnerships with faculty colleagues. Potential topics include the interrelationship of student development and student learning, how to apply learning-centered practices such as providing each student with a road map of how to become a more active and engaged learner, and how student affairs–based programs contribute to student learning and success. After stimulating a collegewide dialogue by asking all areas how their work contributed to student learning, the Maricopa Community Colleges established a Student Services Institute to help student affairs professionals strengthen their understanding of a variety of topics, including the philosophy and core values of the student affairs profession, theory and research related to student retention and success, contemporary legal issues, and opportunities for partnerships between academic and student affairs colleagues (Kushibab, 2005).

Step 3: Ground Partnerships in Real Institutional Problems and Opportunities. Community colleges must make sure that student and academic affairs partnerships address *real* institutional problems and opportunities. Advisory committees and liaison relationships that do not address real challenges are often unproductive and provide only the appearance of collaboration. Because there is no lack of compelling and important issues that can be addressed through effective partnerships, community college leaders should have no difficulty in identifying such challenges and asking for workable solutions from cross-functional groups. For example, increasing student success and retention in developmental courses, narrowing the achievement gap among racial and ethnic student cohorts, increasing the student transfer rate from community colleges to four-year institutions, facilitating deeper student learning through service learning, and measuring student learning through an institution-wide assessment program are great challenges worthy of consideration by the best and brightest minds in both academic and student affairs. The effectiveness of partnerships in dealing with real challenges is illustrated by the orientation course for first-year students developed by academic and student affairs colleagues at Pierce College in Washington. This program increased students' understanding of their learning styles, their ability to use different learning strategies, and their knowledge of support services such as tutoring and services for students with disabilities (Community College Survey of Student Engagement, 2003).

Step 4: Leverage the Assessment Movement. Developing and using learning outcomes for student affairs program improvement are essential in demonstrating student affairs professionals' contributions to student learning. As colleges address challenges in increasing student success in remedial courses, student affairs assessment and outcomes data can be used to support student learning. For example, learning support center professionals can work with mathematics faculty to develop learning outcomes for tutoring that are linked to course competencies. As well, student life practitioners can use speech communication rubrics developed by faculty members to evaluate student leadership presentations, and financial aid staff can use English composition rubrics developed by their faculty colleagues to evaluate the quality of scholarship essays. In addition, assessment center staff can provide valuable information to faculty members about students' problem-solving skills and learning styles. Through partnerships with faculty, student affairs professionals can develop effective out-of-class learning outcomes and measurement tools.

Step 5: Modify Organizational Structures to Facilitate Collaboration. Adjusting the organizational and physical structures where faculty and student affairs professionals interact can help facilitate collaboration. Effective strategies include inviting the senior student affairs officer to play a meaningful role in appropriate academic affairs committees and standing meetings, inviting faculty to have meaningful leadership roles in traditional student affairs functional areas, and developing shared leadership on college task forces and committees. At Austin Community College (Texas), faculty members serve on hiring committees for important student affairs positions, provide input into the development of student affairs programs, evaluate student affairs programs, and participate in program reviews (Culp, 2001). Several of the community colleges in the Maricopa system recently decided to provide faculty release or overload time to assist student affairs staff in developing student learning outcomes and to align outcomes assessment both in and outside the classroom.

Step 6: Realign Budget Allocations to Support Collaboration. Community college administrators must realign the budget allocation process to increase collaborative efforts between academic and student affairs practitioners. Similarly, student affairs leaders can allocate some of their financial resources to support academic initiatives. Student life programs can align their offerings (such as guest speakers, films, musical presentations) with collegewide learning themes, support student academic events such as essay or art competitions, and assist with the accomplishment of collegewide initiatives such as diversity programming. For example, the Maricopa Community Colleges' Diversity Infusion Program (http://www.maricopa.edu/diversityinfusion/) uses student diversity interns to assist faculty with integrating diversity into the curriculum. At several colleges in the Maricopa system, these interns are recruited and financially supported by student affairs.

Challenges in Creating Partnerships

Despite the benefits of collaborative partnerships between academic and student affairs divisions, many barriers impede such collaborations. These include differing cultures, values, and skill sets, structural hierarchical separation, differing program outcomes (affective versus cognitive), lack of a common language, different organizational status, and lack of connection between the curriculum and cocurriculum (Banta and Kuh, 1998; Kezar, 2003; Schroeder, 1998). The cultural and communication barriers may be attributed to differences in professional preparation, lack of shared journal readings, and the disconnect between student development and academic content–based research. Although these barriers have long and deep historical roots tied to the organizational structures in higher education, a number of other challenges emerge from the everyday culture of the community college. For example, faculty and student affairs professionals are generally not located proximately, and thus casual and spontaneous interaction is infrequent. As well, student affairs administrators are rarely included in academic division leadership meetings on a regular basis, and faculty members generally do not take part in student affairs meetings. In some cases, professional development occurs in a segregated fashion, with faculty and student affairs staff engaged in separate learning opportunities.

Nevertheless, these challenges to collaboration can and have been overcome to create strategic and intentional partnerships between student and academic affairs that enhance student success and student learning. For example, at Paradise Valley Community College, faculty and staff development (and their budgets) have been merged under the umbrella of the Employee and Organizational Learning Team (http://www.pvc.maricopa. edu/eol). This team is composed of both faculty and staff, and professional development programs are open to all campus personnel. In addition, professional development topics are presented in the context of both student and academic affairs practice.

Partnerships in Practice

Schroeder (1998) suggests that a number of programs "straddle" student and academic affairs units, and argues that these programs are ideal for meaningful collaborations and partnerships. Several community colleges have created exemplary partnerships in eight of these areas.

First-Year Experience Programs. Community college First-Year Experience (FYE) programs include student and academic support services that can enhance student success during the first year in college. FYE activities are often embedded in course content, and include cocurricular activities that help students navigate their first year of college. At Paradise Valley Community College, for example, collaboration between faculty and student affairs professionals resulted in an innovative FYE program built around the learning community model (http://www.pvc.maricopa.edu/ ~fye/). Cohorts of students enroll in two or three linked courses that provide opportunities for study groups, peer tutoring, faculty interaction, integration of assignments, group projects, and development of team-building skills. Paradise Valley's FYE program also includes cocurricular elements such as student gatherings, information about financial aid, testing, computer and library services, and tutoring. Participation in the FYE program significantly increases student retention. For example, during the 2002–03 academic year, 95 percent of FYE students completed the cohort block, 91 percent enrolled in second-semester courses (compared with 83 percent in the overall student body), and 81 percent enrolled in a college-credit course the following fall (compared with the collegewide average of 55 percent).

Early Intervention Programs. Faculty and student affairs staff should collaborate on early intervention programs to engage students with support services and staff as early as possible, and before crises develop. Middlesex Community College (Massachusetts), for example, developed collaborative intervention teams to work with at-risk students. Including representatives from the student development, academic affairs, academic resources, and institutional planning and research divisions, the intervention teams were created to increase collaboration between student and academic affairs, engage students before crises developed, and improve course completion rates. The teams use intervention strategies to address early awareness of problems, assess study skills and learning styles, and promote connections with students. In 1999 math course completion rates were 5 percent higher for students involved with an intervention team, and retention rates from one semester to the next were 9 percent higher (National Association of Student Personnel Administrators and National Council on Student Development, 2003).

Learning Communities. Learning communities consist of linked or integrated courses centered on a common theme, and offer opportunities to link the classroom to activities like service learning and cocurricular programming. Student affairs staff can become meaningfully involved in integrating student success strategies and cocurricular programming such as goal setting and personal development in learning communities. The Math Express to Success program at Phoenix College (Arizona) has developed a learning community that compresses three algebra courses into one semester (http://www.pc.maricopa.edu/Mathematics/MathExpress.html). Designed for small cohorts ranging from fifteen to twenty students, Math Express puts students into three- to four-person teams for practice, tutoring, and peer teaching. In addition, participants receive targeted academic advising, financial aid, and mentoring support services (Community College Survey of Student Engagement, 2003).

Service Learning. By collaborating on service-learning projects, student affairs staff can integrate a student's community service or volunteer experience into an academic course. Student affairs professionals generally provide the logistical support for service-learning activities, which often means arranging for service sites in the community, providing orientation for students, and helping run professional development programs for faculty on how to incorporate service learning into the curriculum. The Houston Community College System (Texas) has developed a service-learning program that helps students enhance their intellectual and social skills, gain real-world experience, and develop a commitment to social problems facing the community (http://www.hccs.edu/system/Instructional_Services/serLrning/serLrning.html). Student affairs staff members assist faculty in writing grant applications, conducting orientation sessions, facilitating reflection sessions, and participating in project reviews and evaluations. Students in this program have participated in over twenty thousand hours of service over the past five years (Community College Survey of Student Engagement, 2003).

Distance Education Programs. Providing support services for distance and online learners is an emerging arena for partnerships between academic and student affairs. Student affairs professionals can provide specialized online learner readiness inventories via interactive Web sites, establish retention programs using follow-up telephone calls, and provide innovative tutoring programs such as "beep-a-tutor," where tutors are available to distance learners via paging or cell phone technology. For example, Rio Salado College (Arizona) follows a systems approach to student learning where employees no longer function exclusively in their segregated departments. Instead, employees in every college area are centered on the student and provide support for learning. Rio Salado provides all major services over the Internet, including registration, textbook orders, academic advising and counseling, tutoring, and applications for financial aid. Academic and student affairs personnel collaborate extensively on designing and implementing programs and services. As a result of this collaboration, Rio Salado College has carved out a market niche as a leading distance learning provider and has experienced annual double-digit growth in online enrollment (Thor and Scarafiotti, 2004).

Academic Advising. Academic advising, which includes assisting students with setting clear educational goals and developing academic plans, provides another opportunity for student and academic affairs to collaborate. Valencia Community College (Florida) developed its LifeMap program to assist students with an action plan for using college resources. One component of the program is developmental advising (http://valenciacc. edu/lifemap). LifeMap engages the entire college by linking essential components such as faculty, staff, courses, technology, and programs and services to help students succeed in college. LifeMap focuses on improving students' self-confidence, decision making, and self-sufficiency (Community College Survey of Student Engagement, 2004). As a result, the semester-to-semester persistence rates for Valencia students increased from 65 percent in 1994–95 to 79 percent in 2003–04 (Romano, 2004). Valencia Community College has also experienced increases in enrollment, course completion rates, graduation rates, and transfer rates into state universities, and currently awards more associate degrees than any other community college in the United States (Romano, 2004).

Academic Bridge Programs. At many colleges, high school bridge programs that allow students to receive both college and high school credit are the product of partnerships between academic and student affairs. High school relationships, recruitment, orientation, and mentoring are often provided by student affairs practitioners, and counselors and student affairs coordinators are often assigned to individual classes to implement cocurricular activities linked to course outcomes. In 2002, Estrella Mountain

Community College (Arizona) implemented the NASA Center for Success in Math and Science as the college's core driver for student success in mathematics and science (http://www.emc.maricopa.edu/academics/nasacenter/). The center provides K–12 outreach programs designed to inspire students to pursue education in math and the sciences, community college support programs that work with faculty to support learning both in and out of the classroom, and several additional programs. One of the goals for the program was to increase college course completion rates from 70 to 75 percent by the year 2006. With the support and contributions of the NASA Center programs, the college reached its 75 percent goal in 2003–04.

Conflict Management Services. Academic and student affairs personnel share the challenge of helping students without strong conflict management skills learn how to resolve conflicts. Madison Area Technical College (Wisconsin) offers conflict management services to assist with both informal and formal mediation. Focusing on student code-of-conduct issues, grading disputes, interpersonal conflicts, discrimination and harassment, and nonacademic student grievances, the program helps students learn conflict management skills and strategies. Results of the program have been very positive. In 2002, eighty cases were referred to the conflict management program (fifty-eight by students, twenty-two by faculty). Seventy-eight percent of the cases were resolved informally through the mediation process, 10 percent were resolved formally through the school's Judicial Review Board or Academic Appeals Committee, and 12 percent were resolved through outside services (National Association of Student Personnel Administrators and National Council on Student Development, 2003).

The Importance of Technology in Enhancing Partnerships

Discussions about educational technology on community college campuses no longer center on when and if to use it. The focus is now on how to incorporate technology seamlessly into the teaching and learning process (Milliron and Miles, 2000). Technology is viewed as an investment in student learning, one that ensures that a community college education is not limited by time or place. Technology is a tool that can be used to improve the efficiency and effectiveness of student affairs programs, and a bridge that will lead to innovative partnerships between student affairs and academic affairs that help support student learning. Early warning systems, for example, use technology to help personnel from the two divisions identify students at risk of dropping out and intervene in order to assist them in meeting their educational goals.

Several other technology-based collaborations exist between academic and student affairs, including computerized testing to assess learning styles, interest inventories, academic skills assessment for course placement, and assessing learning outcomes for courses. Additional areas of collaboration include electronic prerequisite checking and enforcement, tracking with-drawal patterns for classes and programs, tracking student success to meet the demand for public accountability, and creating degree audit systems that assist students in meeting graduation and degree requirements.

Student demand for technology has influenced the need for online self-service options to assist with registration, orientation, grade checking, and applications for graduation. Technology provides students with the options of taking courses at a distance, receiving online tutoring, and taking part in virtual counseling and advising services that can help them set educational goals and select a program of study. Students use electronic means of com-munication more than ever before, and student and academic affairs pro-fessionals must begin to employ these new communication styles to reach out to students. Just as more faculty are infusing technology into the class-room and using tools such as course management systems that allow for the online posting of class assignments and announcements, student affairs practitioners must use technology to redesign or replace existing services and create new programs to meet the needs of today's students.

Student affairs practitioners can use technology to build additional partnerships not only with academic affairs but with other divisions across the college. To encourage such partnerships, community college leaders may need to consider providing wireless campuses, creating cybercafes, ensuring that help desks are available after the traditional workday ends, and developing a recovery plan for when the technology system goes down. Despite all the advantages technology provides, however, it is important that community college student affairs practitioners continue to cultivate human connections with students, "to ensure that people connect with people on deep and multiple levels" (Milliron and Miles, 2000, p. 18).

Conclusion

Although there are many challenges in creating partnerships between aca-demic and student affairs divisions at community colleges, student affairs professionals have a number of resources to assist them in constructing organizational frameworks that increase such collaborations and enhance the student learning environment. An important next step is to begin to assess more systemically whether existing collaborative programs actually improve student learning and success. Programs that enhance student learn-ing and success should be supported and strengthened, and programs that do not should be discontinued, with the resources that support them redi-rected to successful programs.

Systemically assessing the effects of student and academic partnerships on student learning and success should include gathering institutional data about students, evaluating program and institutional effectiveness, con-ducting surveys and focus groups, evaluating resource allocations, and assessing student learning outcomes. Culp (2003) explains the importance of compiling data on program and institutional effectiveness in a user-friendly format, distributing the information to faculty, staff, and administrators, and using the information to make decisions. Additional data may be collected quantitatively through student and employee surveys, including national student engagement surveys, satisfaction surveys, or surveys particular to a specific institution. Student and employee focus groups can provide descriptive data on the outcomes associated with enhanced partnerships. Finally, it is necessary to evaluate resource allocations to support collaborative learning objectives. Student affairs and academic affairs leaders should also develop student learning outcomes associated with their collaborative partnerships and assess their success in meeting those outcomes. Coupling the knowledge, skills, and perspectives of student affairs and academic affairs professionals also will help institutions define student outcomes, identify strategies to achieve those outcomes, determine how they will be measured, and use data to strengthen partnerships between the two divisions.

References

American Association for Higher Education, American College Personnel Association, and National Association of Student Personnel Administrators. *Powerful Partnerships: A Shared Responsibility for Learning.* Washington, D.C.: American Association for Higher Education, American College Personnel Association, and National Association of Student Personnel Administrators, 1998. http://www.aahe.org/assessment/joint.htm. Accessed May 12, 2005.

American Council on Education. "The Student Personnel Point of View." In G. T. Saddlemire and A. L. Rents (eds.), *Student Affairs: A Profession's Heritage: Significant Articles, Authors, Issues and Documents.* Carbondale, Ill.: American College Personnel Association, 1983.

Banta, T., and Kuh, G. "A Missing Link in Assessment: Collaboration Between Academic and Student Affairs Professionals." *Change,* Mar.-Apr. 1998, 40–46.

Community College Survey of Student Engagement. "Engaging Community Colleges: National Benchmarks of Quality: 2003 Findings." Austin, Tex.: Community College Survey of Student Engagement, 2003.

Community College Survey of Student Engagement. "Engagement by Design: 2004 Findings." Austin, Tex.: Community College Survey of Student Engagement, 2004.

Cross, K. P. "What Do We Know About Students' Learning and How Do We Know It?" Paper presented at the national conference of the American Association for Higher Education, Cincinnati, Ohio, June 1998. http://www.aahe.org/nche/cross_lecture.htm. Accessed May 12, 2005.

Culp, M. M. "Infiltrating Academe." In M. M. Culp and S. R. Helfgot (eds.), *Life at the Edge of the Wave: Lessons from the Community College.* Washington, D.C.: National Association of Student Personnel Administrators, 1998.

Culp, M. M. "Managing Change Without Destroying Staff, Students, or Student Affairs." Paper presented at the American College Personnel Association convention, Boston, Mar. 2001.

Culp, M. M. "What Matters in Helping Student Success at the Maricopa Community Colleges." Paper presented at the Success Conference sponsored by the Maricopa Community College District, Scottsdale, Ariz., Oct. 2003.

Dale, P. "A Journey in Becoming More Learning-Centered." *NASPA Net Results,* Nov. 11, 2003, n.p.

Ewell, P. "Organizing for Learning: A Point of Entry. Draft Prepared for Discussion at the American Association for Higher Education Summer Academy." Boulder, Colo.: National Center for Higher Education Management Systems, 1997. http://www.intime. uni.edu/model/learning/learn_summary.html. Accessed May 10, 2005.

Flynn, W. "The Learning Decade." *Learning Abstracts*, 2003, *6*(1), n.p.

Harvey, L., and Knight P. *Transforming Higher Education*. London: Open University Press, 1996.

Kezar, A. "Achieving Student Success: Strategies for Creating Partnerships Between Academic and Student Affairs." *NASPA Journal*, 2003, *41*(1), 1–22.

Kinzie, J., and Kuh, G. "Going Deep: Learning from Campuses That Share Responsibility for Student Success." *About Campus*, 2004, *9*(5), 2–8.

Kushibab, D. "Community College Student Services Institute." Paper presented at the National Association of Student Personnel Administrators convention, Tampa, Fla., Mar. 2005.

League for Innovation in the Community College. "Learning College Project," 2004. http://www.league.org/league/projects/lcp/index.htm. Accessed May 10, 2005.

Maricopa Community College District. "Summary of Governing Board Strategic Conversation. What Really Matters: Student Success, Student Development, and Student Services." Tempe, Ariz.: Maricopa Community College District, 2004.

McClenney, K. M. "Keeping America's Promise: Challenges for Community Colleges." In K. Boswell and C. D. Wilson (eds.), *Keeping America's Promise: A Report on the Future of the Community College*. Denver: Education Commission of the States and the League for Innovation in the Community College, 2004. http://www.communitycollegepolicy.org/pdf/KeepingAmericasPromise.pdf. Accessed Jul. 6, 2005.

Milliron, M., and Miles, C. *Taking a Big Picture Look at Technology, Learning, and the Community College*. Mission Viejo, Calif.: League for Innovation in the Community College, 2000.

National Association of Student Personnel Administrators and National Council on Student Development. "Exemplary Program: Bridges to Student Success." Washington, D.C.: National Association of Student Personnel Administrators and National Council on Student Development, 2003.

O'Banion, T. *Creating More Learning-Centered Colleges*. Mission Viejo, Calif.: League for Innovation in the Community College, 1997.

O'Banion, T. *Launching a Learning-Centered College*. Mission Viejo, Calif.: League for Innovation in the Community College, 1999.

Paradise Valley Community College. "An Advocacy Position Concerning Underprepared Students at PVCC." Phoenix, Ariz.: Paradise Valley Community College, 2004.

Romano, J. C. "LifeMap: A Learning-Centered System for Student Success." Paper presented at the National Council on Student Development annual conference, Orlando, Fla., Oct. 2004.

Schroeder, C. "Developing Collaborative Partnerships That Enhance Student Learning and Educational Attainment: Higher Education Trends for the Next Century," 1998. http://www.acpa.nche.edu/seniorscholars/trends/trends7.htm. Accessed May 10, 2005.

Senge, P. *The Fifth Discipline Fieldbook*. New York: Doubleday, 1994.

Thor, L., and Scarafiotti, C. "Mainstreaming Distance Learning into the Community College." *Journal of Asynchronous Learning Networks*, 2004, *8*(1), 1–11.

PAUL A. DALE *is dean of learning support services at Paradise Valley Community College in Arizona.*

TONYA M. DRAKE *is district director for student development services at the Maricopa Community Colleges in Arizona.*

5

This chapter describes two emerging theories that inform career counseling and explores how they can strengthen student success programs for underrepresented populations. The chapter also describes several effective programs and services that support traditionally underrepresented students as they prepare for, succeed in, and make the transition out of the community college.

Using Theory and Research to Improve Student Affairs Practice: Some Current Examples

Dawn R. Person, Pilar Ellis, Caryn Plum, Debra Boudreau

For many students, community colleges are the point of entry into the higher education system. Although some educators argue that students who attend community colleges are less likely to obtain a bachelor's degree than those who enroll directly in four-year institutions (Schneider and Stevenson, 1999), for many students from underrepresented populations, the choice is not between two- or four-year colleges but between the community college and no college (Cohen and Brawer, 1996). Many community college students are the first in their families to attend college, immigrants, returning adults, or members of an underrepresented population based on their ethnicity, cultural orientation, or socioeconomic status (Bailey, 2004). Often, these students have a limited understanding of how to succeed in higher education and lack essential academic skills, thus presenting significant challenges to the institution. In order to help these students define and reach their educational and career goals, community college student affairs professionals, especially those with responsibility for providing career counseling services and increasing student access to higher education, must move beyond traditional models of student learning and development and incorporate a social perspective such as that proposed by Tanaka (2002). Tanaka suggests that social theory is the missing link between student development theory and effective programs and services that can benefit all students, including those considered nontraditional in higher education.

This chapter begins by describing the gap between research, theory, and practice in career counseling, then details two emerging theories—social theory and relational theory—that build on traditional notions of student development to improve practice in community colleges. The chapter then describes several effective programs and services that support traditionally underrepresented students as they prepare for, succeed in, and transition out of the community college.

Theory and Practice in Career Counseling

One of the most frequently cited strengths of career counseling is that its practice has been informed by many theories and extensive research on career development processes (Harris-Bowlsbey, 2003; Savickas, 2003; Tang, 2003; Whiston, 2003). Flores, Scott, Wang, and Yakushko (2003), in their review of research on career theory, identify five categories of career development theories: person-environment, developmental, social cognitive, social learning, and career decision-making theories. Person-environment theories take into account an individual's personal variables, such as interests, skills, and aptitudes, and assess their fit with environmental factors of the workplace. Perhaps one the most significant influences on career counseling has been the use of Holland's RIASEC model (1984), which classifies personality types and environmental factors of the workplaces as *realistic, investigative, artistic, social, enterprising,* and *conventional* (Flores, Scott, Wang, and Yakushko, 2003). Developmental theories primarily focus on Super's lifespan theory (1990), explore career development at different stages of life, and integrate multiple life roles. Social cognitive and social learning theories examine how interactions among personal, environmental, and behavioral variables affect career choices. Career decision-making theories include Frank Parsons's work (1909) on career indecisiveness and occupational choice (Flores, Scott, Wang, and Yakushko, 2003).

Despite the wealth of theory pertaining to career development and choice processes, there is a gap between theory and community college practice (Niles, 2003; Savickas, 2003; Tang, 2003; Whiston, 2003). Niles (2003) argues that this occurs because many career theories describe the career development process rather than focusing on interventions that will help clients, and contends that career counselors need a better understanding of the specific techniques and interventions that are most effective with particular clients. Whiston (2003) argues that this gap occurs because, "contrary to other counseling fields, the theoretical models in career counseling have not evolved to the point where it is possible to say Theory A is better than Theory B with a specific group" (p. 40). Recognizing the discrepancy between what researchers study and what practitioners use, several scholars have called for further research about the career counseling process as well as outcomes of the process for particular groups of students in order to reduce the gap between theory and practice.

Research and theory on career development and counseling processes that take into account the needs of specific groups of students are particularly important in the two-year college because a significant number of community college students are undecided about their career and educational goals and thus may not be well served by traditional theories. For example, Healy and Reilly (as cited in Grubb, 2001) point out that older students interested in changing careers, as well as first-generation students who have little understanding of higher education and its connection to career development, may have different needs than more traditional college students. Student affairs professionals in community colleges must provide effective career counseling services to a student population with a variety of needs, backgrounds, and levels of preparation. To do so requires increased attention to research about the importance of ethnic and cultural sensitivity, as well as an understanding of emerging theories that consider the importance of students' relationships with others. When student affairs professionals incorporate this research and theory into their career counseling models, career counseling becomes a more individualized, holistic process that explores community college students' identity development, cultural values, and social interactions.

Emerging Theories of Career Development

Given the diversity of the community college student population, as well as the diversity of the country's changing workforce, many scholars argue that career development models must pay greater attention to students' social and cultural backgrounds and needs, and to the importance of students' relationships with others. The following sections examine two emerging theories that can be applied to career development and counseling: social theory and relational theory.

Social Theory. According to Teng, Morgan, and Anderson (2001), ethnicity is "a statistically significant factor in identifying differences in community college students' career development, particularly in their career goals and career preparation actions" (p. 123). However, as Brown (2000) found, most existing career development theories do not emphasize cultural sensitivity. He argues that many theories about career choice emphasize independent decision making, even though many minority groups use a collective social value and place a greater emphasis on the wants and needs of the community. Although Lent and Worthington (2000) caution that Brown fails to acknowledge within-group variability and thus "runs the risk of perpetuating cultural uniformity assumptions or stereotypes" (p. 379), several scholars and practitioners agree that career development theories should better incorporate sensitivity for individual students' social and cultural backgrounds and needs.

Tanaka's social theory (2002) is one framework that incorporates a focus on culture. Tanaka suggests that, by building on the theories of Tinto,

Pace, and Astin about how and why students succeed in college (academic and social integration, effort expended in learning, and campus involvement, respectively), social theory offers new insights and can strengthen traditional notions of student and career development theory in the context of modern American colleges. Specifically, Tanaka advocates an inclusive model of student development that relies on the concept of individual *voice* in order to embrace the cultures of students historically excluded from higher education and thus not included in traditional theories of student and career development. He argues that culture should be a central theme in these theories, because gender, race, sexuality, ability, and socioeconomic status are highly salient to students. Culture should also be made central to student affairs program development and service delivery.

According to Tanaka (2002), in social theory "the interactions between student, college, student major, family, and close friends and society are all considered important" (p. 284). The college experience is not viewed as a monolithic process that all students experience but as many different experiences that occur on a college campus given the difference in students and their interactions with the college environment. Tanaka's approach allows for multiple perspectives of student and career development and "considers issues of culture and power" (p. 285) in the community college. It requires that all students be heard and understood and that the types of questions asked should elicit responses that encourage multiple voices and perspectives. This approach recognizes and values each student's goals and expectations. In addition, Tanaka suggests revamping widely used instruments that measure student development in college in order to be more inclusive of culture. At the core of this intercultural approach is a holistic perspective of the student that, in reality, is the foundation of the student affairs profession.

If student affairs professionals applied Tanaka's approach, Chickering and Reisser's vectors of student identity development (1993) would not only consider campus size and students' interactions with the environment but would also measure student behavior in a multidimensional cultural context. For example, a low-income student of color would be understood and valued in the cultural context that she brings to the college experience, not necessarily in comparison to what might be considered the "norm." Career counselors, as well as all student affairs professionals, should aim to connect programming and services to emerging theories, such as Tanaka's, that recognize multidimensional cultural contexts.

Relational Theory. In addition to paying greater attention to students' cultural and ethnic backgrounds and needs, community college career counselors would benefit from incorporating another emerging theory, relational connectedness, into their practice. According to Schultheiss (2003), individualism and independent thought have long been the central forces in many career theories. Given the strong reliance on personal variables such as those included in Holland's typology, much of career development theory has focused on autonomous individuals and their fit into a career. However, this viewpoint fails to consider a person's relationships with others and the effects of those relationships on the career choice process. Incorporating relational theory with traditional career development theories provides a more holistic framework and allows community college students to integrate "established career practices with a more sensitive appreciation of the intertwined nature of people's relational and career worlds" (Schultheiss, 2003, p. 303). It can also help students and career counselors be aware of how others (for example, family, mentors, role models, or significant others) can influence career development.

Relational theory has its roots in feminist and social support theories proposed by Gilligan (1982) and Josselson (1992), who believe that our interconnectedness and the relationships we have with others are critical to the development of our own sense of self (Schultheiss, 2003). By emphasizing relationships with others and taking into account individual cultural and ethnic values, career counselors can help community college students see the career process as a complex and individual journey.

By applying relational theory to career development, counselors can explore the types of people who are important to students (for example, parents, siblings, significant others) and begin to understand how these relationships affect the career decision-making process (Schultheiss, 2003). Relational theory also allows counselors to explore the influence of cultural values in this process, and can help students become "better equipped to face relational and career dilemmas, progress effectively within the career domain, effectively draw on relationships with others as resources in the career development process, and benefit from deepened and more meaningful connections with others" (Schultheiss, 2003, p. 305).

Relational theory can easily be applied in the community college. California's Puente project, for example, incorporates relational theory into its day-to-day activities by placing participants in cohorts, organizing learning communities, and linking students to role models in the community (Laden, 1999). Similarly, the national Mathematics Engineering Science Achievement (MESA) program recognizes the importance of relational theory by providing participants with mentors, academic and career counseling, tutoring, research opportunities, internships, weekend summer courses, and culturally sensitive standardized-test preparation.

Although not focused exclusively on community college students, *Career Development and Vocational Behavior of Racial and Ethnic Minorities* (Leong, 1995) is an excellent resource for student affairs practitioners attempting to create career counseling programs that pay more attention to students' cultural backgrounds. A team of national experts offers an overview of the career development needs of many students served by community colleges, discusses assessment and counseling strategies in a cultural context, and explores the interaction of race, ethnicity, and gender, as well as the need for specially focused interventions.

Services for Students Traditionally Underrepresented in Higher Education

Community college student affairs divisions provide many programs and services for students traditionally underrepresented in higher education. Some of these programs simply increase awareness of higher education opportunities, others help students prepare for and succeed in college, and a few are designed to increase awareness of the opportunities available after graduation. All of these programs are excellent examples of what happens when community college student affairs professionals manage to translate theory and research successfully into practice.

College Preparation. Research indicates that the opportunity to attend college is "hollow rhetoric" unless institutions help prospective students understand the importance of higher education and how to navigate the entrance process (Fitzgerald, 2003, p. 3). Many educational leaders also believe that "the last year of high school is a waste" (Schroeder, 2003, p. 8), that high school curricula do not prepare students for college (Jacobson, 2004), and that too many students drop out of school between the ninth and the twelfth grades (Roueche and Roueche, 1993). In many states, community college student affairs practitioners are responding to these challenges by creating programs that increase the chances students will graduate from high school, be prepared for college, and easily navigate the college admission process. The programs are based on student development theory and address issues of competence, purpose, motivation, focus, and achievement.

Over the past few decades, many community colleges have begun collaborating with local high schools to provide innovative programs to students through *middle college high schools,* which allow high school students to enroll in both high school and community college courses. Middle college high schools got their start in 1974 at LaGuardia Community College (New York) and quickly spread throughout the nation. In 2002, there were at least twenty-four middle college high schools in eleven different states (Conley, 2002). Although they differ somewhat in their specific focus and objectives, they all serve to assist students in completing high school and entering college.

LaGuardia Community College's original goal was to reduce dropout rates for all high school students, although recently it has shifted its focus to improving completion rates of recent immigrants. High school sophomores who are in trouble are the focus of a middle college high school program in Las Vegas, Nevada, and "junior and seniors who are creative, artistic, independent thinkers" (Conley, 2002, p. 2) are admitted to a program in San Mateo, California. Second-year high school students in the San Bernardino City Unified School District who have the potential to graduate from high school and attend college but lack the motivation to do so attend San Bernardino Valley Community College (California) for the first half of the day and honors-level high school classes for the second half. These students can earn both a high school diploma and an associate degree at the same time (Borsuk and Vest, 2002).

The outcomes of middle college high schools have been positive. In 1998, middle college high schools reported a student retention rate of 85 percent, with 75 percent of seniors graduating and 78 percent of them going on to college (Lieberman, 1998). The Mott middle college high school in Flint, Michigan, has seen its graduates enroll in two- and four-year colleges at a higher rate than other students, and the middle college high school of Shelby State College in Memphis, Tennessee, has contributed to lower dropout rates and improved test scores at the high school and to enrollment growth at the college (Conley, 2002). Middle college high schools serve a broad range of learners, reduce high school dropout rates, and motivate students to achieve beyond high school and enter college early. Middle college high schools are thus advantageous for learners and effective in retaining students in both high school and college.

Outreach. Many community college outreach programs have been influenced by Rendon's validation theory (2002), which posits that student affairs professionals and faculty need to actively pursue underrepresented students, that these students need to feel they belong in the community college and that their cultures are appreciated. Community colleges must send a direct message to students from diverse backgrounds that they are valued and wanted on campus, and then demonstrate that by providing students with access to faculty members who can serve as mentors and to learning experiences that are respectful and make students feel they matter. Two programs that successfully apply validation theory are the MESA program and the Puente project.

Hartnell College in Salinas, California, has a computer science, engineering, and mathematics (CSEM) program based on the MESA model and collaborates with other campus programs to create an effective infrastructure for student success. In addition to MESA activities such as those described earlier in this chapter, students in the CSEM program are put into cohort clusters and have access to a MESA student center. The CSEM program has increased participants' grade point averages and improved their retention and graduation rates (Kane, Beals, Valeau, and Johnson, 2004).

Thirty-eight community colleges in California have Puente projects that use "a multidimensional, integrative approach" to support the academic development and retention of students. The project also emphasizes Latino culture, which affirms who students are and "what they bring with them to the college" (Laden, 1999, p. 55). Puente places students in intensive freshman English courses, provides counselors in the classrooms, and employs mentors from the Latino professional and academic community (Laden, 1999). By including counselors in the classroom, Puente provides a seamless learning environment for students and a more welcoming orientation to college. Puente creates personal, caring relationships, which help students commit to staying in college, and employs holistic learning, which creates intellectual, social, and emotional development (Rendon, 2002). Research indicates that Puente participants have higher retention and transfer rates, "higher educational attainment and career goals, greater self-confidence, a stronger sense of ethnic identity," and a willingness to assume more leadership roles than students not participating in the program (Laden, 1999, p. 63).

Mentoring. Mentoring programs are successful when they effectively assist students in dealing with day-to-day challenges. Research demonstrates that establishing multilevel mentoring programs that provide guidance to students academically, personally, and professionally increases the likelihood of success for minority students (Pope, 2002). Drawing from this research, St. Petersburg College (Florida) initiated the Brother-to-Brother mentoring program for African American males to help achieve college entrance, academic success, and persistence. Emphasizing positive interactions with faculty and staff, the program provides participants with assessment, early registration, priority scheduling, peer support, and tutoring. Program outcomes include raising student awareness about societal issues and opportunities, increasing faculty and staff awareness of diverse student needs, and contributing to a supportive environment for students (Leach, 2001). Similarly, the Arranged Mentor for Instructional Guidance and Organizational Support (AMIGOS) program offered at many institutions across the country matches mentors and protégés based on personality type, and arranges structured problem-solving opportunities, training sessions, and social activities to assist students making the transition into the college environment (Pope, 2002).

Transfer Services. Transferring to a four-year institution is a goal of many community college students, but research indicates that transfer students "sometimes find it difficult to adjust to an environment that offers less personal attention from faculty and staff than that available at most two-year institutions" (Frost, 1991, p. 51). Based on this and related research, several community colleges work to help students understand the full range of opportunities available to them after graduating from a community college. For example, eight community colleges in New York (Dutchess, Hostas, LaGuardia, Orange County, Ulster County, Schenectady County, Westchester, and Borough of Manhattan community colleges) collaborate with Vassar College to sponsor Exploring Transfer, a program that allows community college students to spend five weeks on the Vassar campus, live in residence halls, attend a writing lab, and earn academic credits for two courses, both of which are team-taught by community college and Vassar faculty. In twelve years, 64 percent of the Exploring Transfer students have gone on to earn a four-year degree, and only one student has dropped out of the program (Lieberman, 1998).

Conclusion

This chapter discussed the need for student affairs professionals to embrace social theory as a bridge to student development theory and practice and to develop and become involved in programs that emphasize students' cultures and unique backgrounds and needs. When working with English language learners who are low-income, first-generation college students, for example, student affairs professionals must understand and respond to all aspects of these learners and connect them to programs and services that are accessible and responsive to their unique needs, not the needs of the institution. As well, student affairs professionals must help their institutions ask and answer five essential questions: Who are we serving? Are we meeting the needs of these students? What populations in the community are we not serving? Why are we not serving these populations? What are the consequences to the college and the community of not serving these students? These questions—especially the last three—can lead to an open dialogue among faculty, staff, and administrators, and can provide an opportunity to explore new programs and services to meet students' changing needs while ensuring flexibility of service design and delivery.

Community college student affairs practitioners must also act on research that allows for student input and investment and that demonstrates that students gain from being actively involved in college and in the learning process. Further, they must offer programs designed to foster this engagement. In order to truly meet students' complex needs, practitioners must engage students and assist them in becoming authors of their own educational experience. This requires student affairs professionals to view students at the center of the learning experience and help them find a strong voice to influence institutional policy and program development. When this occurs, each student becomes an expert in his or her own learning process and development, and relies on past experiences and future goals for direction. Student affairs professionals will continue to support, direct, and educate students, yet all activities will be carried out *with* rather than *for* students.

Despite recent studies on community college students and a few emerging theories about student development, further theoretical and scholarly research is critical. To be successful, community colleges must meet students' needs by paying attention to new theories and research that can help them serve an ever-changing population of students and respond to local and national economic and workforce needs. Community colleges should embrace Tanaka's social theory (2002), which insists on all voices being heard and understood, as well as relational theory, which can reveal the nature of relationships and learning in the context of culture and community.

References

Bailey, T. "Community College Students: Characteristics, Outcomes, and Recommendations for Success." *Community College Research Center Currents,* Apr. 2004, pp. 1–3.

Borsuk, C., and Vest, B. "Reaching Higher: Secondary Interventions." *Leadership,* 2002, 32(2), 16–18.

Brown, D. "Theory and the School-to-Work Transition: Are the Recommendations Suitable for Cultural Minorities?" *Career Development Quarterly,* 2000, 48(4), 370–375.

Chickering, A. W., and Reisser, L. *Education and Identity* (2nd ed.). San Francisco: Jossey-Bass, 1993.

Cohen, A. M., and Brawer, F. B. *The American Community College* (3rd ed.). San Francisco: Jossey-Bass, 1996.

Conley, D. T. "Preparing Students for Life After High School." *Educational Leadership,* 2002, 59(7), 60–63.

Fitzgerald, B. K. "The Opportunity for a College Education: Real Promise or Hollow Rhetoric?" *About Campus,* 2003, 8(5), 3–10.

Flores, L. Y., Scott, A. B., Wang, Y., and Yakushko, O. "Practice and Research in Career Counseling and Development, 2002." *Career Development Quarterly,* 2003, 52(2), 98–131.

Frost, S. H. *Academic Advising for Student Success: A System of Shared Responsibility.* ASHE-ERIC Higher Education Report No. 3. Washington, D.C.: George Washington University, School of Education and Human Development, 1991.

Gilligan, C. *In a Different Voice.* Cambridge, Mass.: Harvard University Press, 1982.

Grubb, W. N. "Getting into the World: Guidance and Counseling in Community Colleges." New York: Columbia University, Teachers College, Community College Research Center, 2001. (ED 455 880)

Harris-Bowlsbey, J. "A Rich Past and a Future Vision." *Career Development Quarterly,* 2003, 52(1), 18–25.

Holland, J. L. *Making Vocational Choices: A Theory of Personalities and Work Environments.* Englewood Cliffs, N.J.: Prentice Hall, 1984.

Jacobson, J. "High School Curricula Do Not Prepare Students for College." *Chronicle of Higher Education,* Oct. 29, 2004, p. A38.

Josselson, R. *The Space Between Us: Exploring the Dimensions of Human Relationships.* San Francisco: Jossey-Bass, 1992.

Kane, M. A., Beals, C., Valeau, E. J., and Johnson, M. J. "Fostering Success Among Traditionally Underrepresented Student Groups: Hartnell College's Approach to Implementation of the Math Engineering and Science Achievement (MESA) Program." *Community College Journal of Research and Practice,* 2004, 28, 17–26.

Laden, B. V. "Socializing and Mentoring College Students of Color: The Puente Project as an Exemplary Celebratory Socialization Model." *Journal of Higher Education,* 1999, 74(2), 55–74.

Leach, E. J. "Brother-to-Brother: Enhancing the Intellectual and Personal Growth of African-American Males." *Learning Abstracts,* 2001, 4(3). http://www.league.org/publication/abstracts/learning/lelabs0111.html. Accessed May 19, 2005.

Lent, R. W., and Worthington, R. L. "On School-to-Work Transition, Career Development Theories, and Cultural Validity." *Career Development Quarterly,* 2000, 48(4), 376–384.

Leong, F. T. (ed.). *Career Development and Vocational Behavior of Racial and Ethnic Minorities.* Mahwah N.J.: Erlbaum, 1995.

Lieberman, J. "Creating Structural Change: Best Practices." In D. McGrath (ed.), *Creating and Benefiting from Institutional Collaboration: Models for Success.* New Directions for Community Colleges, no. 103. San Francisco: Jossey-Bass, 1998.

Niles, S. G. "Career Counselors Confront a Critical Crossroad: A Vision of the Future." *Career Development Quarterly,* 2003, *52*(1), 70–77.

Parsons, F. *Choosing a Vocation.* Boston: Houghton Mifflin, 1909.

Pope, M. L. "Community College Mentoring: Minority Student Perception." *Community College Review,* 2002, *30*(3), 31–46.

Rendon, L. I. "Community College Puente: A Validating Model of Education." *Educational Policy,* 2002, *16*(4), 642–667.

Roueche, J. E., and Roueche, S. D. *Between a Rock and a Hard Place: The At-Risk Student in the Open-Door College.* Washington, D.C.: Community College Press, 1993.

Savickas, M. L. "Advancing the Career Counseling Profession: Objectives and Strategies for the Next Decade." *Career Development Quarterly,* 2003, *52*(1), 87–96.

Schneider, B., and Stevenson, D. *The Ambitious Generation: America's Teenagers Motivated but Directionless.* New Haven, Conn.: Yale University Press, 1999.

Schroeder, C. "The First Years and Beyond—Charles Schroeder Talks to John Gardner." *About Campus,* 2003, *8*(4), 9–16.

Schultheiss, D. E. "A Relational Approach to Counseling: Theoretical Integration and Practical Application." *Journal of Counseling and Development,* 2003, *81*(3), 301–310.

Super, D. E. "A Life-Span, Life-Space Approach to Career Development." In D. Brown and L. Brooks (eds.), *Career Choice and Development: Applying Contemporary Theories to Practice.* San Francisco: Jossey-Bass, 1990.

Tanaka, G. K. "Higher Education's Self-Reflexive Turn: Toward an Intercultural Theory of Student Development." *Journal of Higher Education,* 2002, *73*(2), 263–296.

Tang, M. "Career Counseling in the Future: Constructing, Collaborating, Advocating." *Career Development Quarterly,* 2003, *52*(1), 61–69.

Teng, L. Y., Morgan, G. A., and Anderson, S. K. "Career Development Among Ethnic and Age Groups of Community College Students." *Journal of Career Development,* 2001, *28*(2), 115–127.

Whiston, S. C. "Career Counseling: 90 Years Old yet Still Healthy and Vital." *Career Development Quarterly,* 2003, *52*(1), 35–42.

DAWN R. PERSON *is professor at California State University, Long Beach, and codirector of the University of California, Irvine, and California State University's joint doctorate program in educational administration and leadership.*

PILAR ELLIS, CARYN PLUM, *and* DEBRA BOUDREAU *are graduates of the master's program in student development in higher education in the department of educational psychology administration and counseling at California State University, Long Beach.*

6

This chapter identifies eleven factors that, when present in a community college, substantially increase the probability that student affairs professionals will be able to create programs that matter to the institution's core mission. The chapter also provides student affairs practitioners with tools to assess the climate in student affairs as well as in the institution for both students and student affairs programs. Finally, the chapter offers guidelines that practitioners can use to design student affairs programs that matter.

Doing More of What Matters: The Key to Student Success

Marguerite M. Culp

In the 1960s, student affairs practitioners described themselves as *client-centered* (Rogers, 1961). In the decades that followed, the term *student-centered* replaced *client-centered,* but was soon replaced by *customer-centered,* which then gave way to today's preferred term, *learning-centered.* In truth, however, student affairs practitioners have always known that community college students are clients, students, customers, *and* learners, which is why—despite the name changes—practitioners were able to hold fast to the profession's core values: ensuring access and opportunity for all, developing the whole student, providing quality services to meet student needs, believing that all students matter, facilitating student learning and success, and believing in the educational richness and power of the out-of-classroom environment.

Essential Factors That Help Student Affairs Professionals Create Programs That Matter

Although these core values guide practice, many factors influence whether student affairs practitioners can successfully translate them into programs that support learning and help students succeed. Eleven of these factors—detailed in the following sections—are so essential that their absence significantly increases the difficulty of implementing student affairs programs that matter.

Essential Factor 1: Supportive Leadership. A president who understands the role that student affairs practitioners must play in a learning-centered institution, who provides the senior student affairs officer with the same status as the senior academic affairs officer, and who creates an institutional climate that values student affairs programs and services is essential. It is also important to have a senior student affairs officer who has a strong background in student affairs theory and research, is respected by the college community, is able to shape institutional culture and policies, and is in a position to compete effectively for resources. In addition, community colleges are best served by student affairs leaders with well-developed communication skills, the ability to gather and analyze data, a penchant for action, personal and professional courage, and an intelligent management style.

Essential Factor 2: Mission-Driven Organizational Structure. An organizational structure that reflects the community college's mission and affirms the role a student affairs division plays in achieving that mission is important. Institutions must intentionally create a structure where student and academic affairs professionals work together on committees, projects, grant-writing activities, and programs designed to increase student learning and success. The structure must also provide student affairs practitioners with a legitimate role in major planning, programming, space allocation, and budget deliberations as well as opportunities to help shape the college's culture.

Essential Factor 3: Data-Based Culture. Community colleges need to create the expectation that all academic and nonacademic professionals will build cultures of evidence that demonstrate how their programs and services matter to the institution's mission. In addition to providing all areas with clear definitions and expectations, community college leaders must actively assist individuals in departments in asking the right questions, measuring what matters, building cultures of evidence, and sharing data with the college community. Without clear expectations and definitions, faculty and student affairs professionals will create programs and services that they believe are important, but no one will know if these programs contribute in a substantive manner to student learning and success.

Essential Factor 4: Adequate Resources. Resources play a significant role in any college's ability to attract and retain students. In community colleges where resources are provided to programs that demonstrate results, building a culture of evidence is the first step in influencing institutional leaders who control space, approve new positions, and make final budget decisions. A culture of evidence also will make it easier for student affairs divisions to compete for external funds such as grants and donations. The second step in influencing the resource allocation process is for student affairs leaders to distribute existing resources in a manner that maximizes benefits to the institution and demonstrates that all decisions are based on data. Because resources do not always come from inside the community college, the third step is to strengthen student affairs programs by competing successfully for grants, discretionary state funds, and donations. The fourth and final step in influencing the resource allocation process is for student affairs leaders to help create a college culture that rewards student affairs divisions when their programs produce results on measures that matter.

Of course, there is no guarantee that student affairs divisions that follow these steps will receive adequate resources, but there is a guarantee that they will be more competitive in the budget allocation process. Conversely, student affairs programs not based on cultures of evidence, unable to demonstrate a connection between their programs and the institution's mission, and unwilling to make difficult decisions about how to allocate existing resources will continue to be marginalized during the budget development process by academic and nonacademic areas that are able to compete more effectively.

Essential Factor 5: Collaborative Institutional Culture. How the college community views student affairs programs and services matters. Successful practitioners understand this and work hard to shape the perceptions of faculty and staff, helping them understand the important link between student affairs practice, student learning, and institutional effectiveness. But presidents, trustees, and academic leaders must do their part to create campus cultures in which student affairs programs and services are valued and the work of practitioners is recognized, respected, and rewarded.

Essential Factor 6: Learning-Centered Policies and Procedures. Most senior student affairs officers have shelves filled with procedures manuals consisting of page after page of rules and regulations. Some, such as academic standards of progress, contribute to student success; others, such as allowing students to register for classes a week or more after the first class session, often invite students to fail. It is essential that community colleges implement consistent policies and procedures that support learning and student success. Student affairs leaders must help community colleges collect and analyze data about the effectiveness of all policies and procedures, retain those that help students succeed, and eliminate those that put students at risk.

Essential Factor 7: Student Engagement. Programs and services that invite—even force—students to connect with faculty, staff, one another, and academic subject matter are important. Institutions that value student success will seize every opportunity to engage students, both in and out of the classroom, from the day they apply until the day they reach their educational and career goals.

Essential Factor 8: Valued and Well-Trained Staff. It is important that student affairs staff members feel valued and well prepared to do their jobs. Community colleges can send a clear message that student affairs practitioners are valued members of the team by providing them with up-to-date job descriptions, adequate orientation to student affairs theory and to their position, clear information about important issues (such as the institution's mission, philosophy, goals, and major challenges), opportunities to shape significant decisions, access to mentoring and professional development activities, fair evaluation and recognition systems, and time for reflection.

Essential Factor 9: Effective Partnerships. When subject matter specialists (faculty members) partner with learning and human development specialists (student affairs practitioners) to create learning-centered institutions, retention and graduation rates increase. When institutional researchers collaborate with their colleagues in student affairs divisions to build cultures of evidence, the resulting information improves decision making across the college. Internal partnerships matter not only because they improve the environment for students and create much-needed faculty support but also because they strengthen the integrity of the institution.

How community colleges connect with external constituencies—the K–12 system, universities, businesses, government agencies, and community and civic organizations—also matters. Colleges that include student affairs professionals in their bridge-building efforts will keep practitioners grounded in the "real world" and benefit from strong links that can yield great dividends for the community college, including better prepared high school students, a greater number of students entering and completing college, easier transitions for graduates and program completers, and high approval ratings among community members.

Essential Factor 10: Intelligent Use of Technology. Information technology has the power to transform education, but many institutions use it merely to replicate or slightly enhance existing programs and practices in the classroom and in student affairs divisions. How community college leaders view technology matters. Those who understand that technology is a natural change agent—a powerful tool that can transform the institution—will use it to reengineer processes, encourage academic and student affairs partnerships, and reward applications that transform learning, support services, and day-to-day operations. In this way, community college leaders can unleash the power of technology and help their colleges become true learning institutions.

Essential Factor 11: Emphasis on Quality. Clearly, quality—quality experiences, quality people, and quality results—matters. Unfortunately, many community college leaders fail to recognize quality programs and services because they have a difficult time defining their mission, identifying what really matters to that mission, and explaining how they plan to measure what matters. Vague mission statements lead to competing visions, unfocused programming efforts, and claims of quality based on measurements and results that, all too often, are not related to the institution's core mission. Effective programs emerge in community colleges that know who they are and communicate this knowledge in a clear and unambiguous manner to students, faculty members, student affairs practitioners, staff, and the community.

Identifying What Matters and What Is Missing

Astin (1993) believes that "investing a relatively high proportion of institutional expenditures in student services pays off in terms of the number of favorable cognitive and affective outcomes that result" (p. 433). Of course, favorable outcomes are more likely to result if resources are invested in programs that matter. Identifying the programs and services that contribute to the institutional goals of student learning and success—as well as identifying the areas that do not contribute—can help community college and student affairs leaders understand where to direct resources. Before this can happen, however, student affairs practitioners must determine if their college's climate supports the creation of programs that matter, look objectively at the climate practitioners have created in student affairs divisions, and use assessment information to modify the climate in both the institution and student affairs in order to produce more programs and services that matter.

Assess the Climate for Student Affairs Programs. Exhibit 6.1 provides a checklist that community college leaders can use to determine the extent to which they are creating a climate that invites practitioners to design and implement student affairs programs that matter. Community colleges that receive eight or more check marks have managed to create climates that support student affairs programs and encourage practitioners to create student support services that matter. Those that receive five to seven check marks are headed in the right direction but have more work to do if they want to create a climate that truly supports student affairs programs and practitioners. Community colleges that receive fewer than five check marks make it challenging, at best, for student affairs leaders and practitioners to create programs that matter; at worst, these institutions create environments that are toxic to student affairs programs. Institutions that receive fewer than five check marks must improve the campus climate for student affairs programs, recognize the importance of these programs to the educational enterprise, and support the efforts of student affairs practitioners who are struggling to create programs that matter.

Assess the Climate for Student Learning. Supporters of the learning-centered college believe there is a relationship between a strong learning climate for students and an environment that encourages student affairs practitioners to provide programs that matter to student learning and success (O'Banion, 2004). Exhibit 6.2 provides a checklist that community college leaders can use to assess the extent to which their institutions create a learning-centered climate for students. Community colleges with nine or more check marks are creating a learning-centered climate for students, whereas those with six to eight check marks are moving from a traditional climate to one that is learning-centered. Community colleges with five or fewer check marks tend to be more traditional than learning-centered. These community colleges must strengthen the climate for students at their institutions and begin the journey toward creating a learning-centered culture.

Assess the Climate in Student Affairs. Exhibit 6.3 allows student affairs practitioners to assess the climate in their own division and determine its readiness to offer programs that matter. Student affairs divisions with eleven or more check marks have a clear understanding of what matters in student affairs and have managed to establish a positive, professional

Exhibit 6.1. Assessing the Climate for Student Affairs Programs

Check all the statements that apply to your institution.

_____ Has a mission statement that clearly outlines core values.

_____ Policies, decisions, and leadership reflect its mission and values.

_____ Is learning-centered.

_____ Sends clear messages that it values student affairs programs and professionals.

_____ Encourages collaboration between academic and student affairs professionals.

_____ Provides student affairs professionals with real opportunities to influence decisions regarding mission, goals, outcomes, and resource allocation.

_____ Assists student affairs professionals in creating strong, positive relationships with K–12 systems in its service area.

_____ Helps student affairs professionals build strong, positive relationships with colleges and universities.

_____ Encourages student affairs professionals to build strong, positive relationships with business, civic, and community groups.

_____ Requires all members of the college community to gather outcomes data, analyze program effectiveness, and make changes as needed.

Suggested interpretation: 8–10 checks = climate supports student affairs professionals and encourages them to create programs that matter; 5–7 checks = climate may support student affairs professionals and allow them to create programs that matter; 1–4 checks = climate makes it challenging for student affairs professionals to create programs that matter.

climate that increases the chances they will create programs and services that make a difference to the college's core mission. Student affairs divisions with six to ten check marks are moving in the right direction and need to continue building a healthy, effective student affairs division. Student affairs divisions with five or fewer check marks need to strengthen their understanding of what matters in student affairs and improve the climate in the division before attempting to influence campus culture, obtain additional funding, or implement new programs and services.

Unlike the items in Exhibits 6.1 and 6.2, student affairs leaders and practitioners control those on the checklist in Exhibit 6.3. Even divisions with small budgets and limited staff can create mission statements, develop program and staff evaluation procedures, and gather data to document how specific programs contribute to student success. Student affairs divisions can also provide staff with comprehensive job descriptions as well as professional development opportunities, opportunities to influence important decisions in student affairs, and effective internal and external communication systems. The keys to success are to identify what matters, set priorities, and allocate resources to support these priorities. Exhibit 6.3 provides

Exhibit 6.2. Assessing the Climate for Student Learning

Check all the statements that apply to your institution.

_____ Can document who its students are and what they need.

_____ Can document how students change over time while in college.

_____ Can document students' successes after they graduate, transfer, reach their educational goals, or enter the workforce.

_____ Can document when and why some students choose to leave.

_____ Communicates clearly to students what is expected of them.

_____ Communicates clearly to faculty that they are responsible for teaching their subjects, helping students understand how to learn, and connecting students to the support services that will help them succeed.

_____ Creates resources to help students meet expectations and reach their goals.

_____ Aggressively connects students to on- and off-campus resources.

_____ Understands the importance of student engagement and intentionally connects students to one another, faculty, staff, and the college.

_____ Encourages student involvement in cocurricular and extracurricular activities.

_____ Involves students in formulating policies and contributing to decisions that have an impact on student life.

Suggested interpretation: 9–11 checks = a climate that is learning-centered; 6–8 checks = a climate that is moving from traditional to learning-centered; 1–5 checks = a climate that is more traditional than learning-centered.

practitioners with a good starting point in creating effective, learning-centered climates by listing fourteen of the most important internal priorities for a community college student affairs division.

Designing the Future

As O'Banion (1997) notes, community colleges are well positioned to lead a fundamental reform in higher education that focuses on learning and puts students first. In a recent keynote address to the National Council on Student Development, O'Banion (2004) challenged practitioners to abandon traditional ways of conceptualizing and delivering services to students, reconnect with the core of their profession, and help their institutions become more learning-centered. This volume of *New Directions for Community Colleges* is designed to help student affairs practitioners respond to O'Banion's challenge by understanding the connection between student affairs programs and the institution's mission, identifying what matters and what is missing in community college student affairs programs, and recognizing the role student affairs professionals can play in creating learning-centered community colleges. Designing the future also requires student

Exhibit 6.3. Assessing the Climate in a Student Affairs Division

Check all the statements that apply to the student affairs area at your institution.

_____ Has a mission statement that reflects the institution's mission and core values.

_____ Follows planning and evaluation procedures that are clearly defined and understood by the college community.

_____ Is able to demonstrate a clear relationship between its policies, programs, and practices and the college's mission and values.

_____ Is able to demonstrate a clear relationship between its policies, programs, and practices and applicable theories (adult development and learning styles, for example).

_____ Is able to demonstrate *with hard data* that its programs and services are based on documented student, faculty, and institutional needs.

_____ Is able to demonstrate *with hard data* that its policies, programs, and practices contribute to student learning.

_____ Is able to demonstrate *with hard data* that its policies, programs, and practices contribute to student success.

_____ Provides new staff members with up-to-date job descriptions, an orientation to the college and their area of responsibility, and a clear explanation of the college's expectations.

_____ Provides all staff members with opportunities to upgrade their skills.

_____ Provides all staff members with the opportunity to meet with supervisors to set annual goals that clearly relate to institutional goals.

_____ Evaluates staff members each year. A significant part of the evaluation is based on their ability to achieve annual goals.

_____ Offers staff members the opportunity to participate in and influence decisions regarding hiring, the allocation of resources, and the development of goals and outcome measures in student affairs.

_____ Communicates with the college community effectively and in a timely manner.

_____ Provides the college community with opportunities to evaluate programs and services provided by student affairs.

Suggested interpretation: 11–14 checks = a program with a clear understanding of what matters in student affairs; 6–10 checks = a program with some understanding of what matters in student affairs; 1–5 checks = a program that needs to strengthen its understanding of what matters in student affairs.

affairs practitioners to understand the importance of intelligent planning, program review, staff development, communication, and celebration.

Identify What Is Missing. Practitioners can use the assessment instruments included in this chapter to determine if change is needed and identify specific gaps in culture and programming. For example, Exhibits 6.1 and 6.2 can both serve as checklists to help practitioners identify what is missing in their college's culture and as blueprints to help community college leaders reshape existing cultures. Similarly, Exhibit 6.3 allows practitioners to gauge the extent to which they have created a healthy climate in the student affairs area, identify what is missing, and understand what they need to do to strengthen the student affairs division at their community college.

Develop a Strategic Plan. Every student affairs division needs a three- to five-year strategic plan that identifies the direction the division is taking, as well as an annual plan that focuses on goals and outcome measures for the current year. Both must be tied to the community college's strategic plan, define clear goals and indicate how goal achievement will be measured, identify the resources required, and demonstrate how investment in each activity will make an important difference to students, staff, faculty, and the institution itself. Every student affairs practitioner must focus on implementing new programs that matter, modifying existing programs, and continually monitoring staff and program effectiveness. In addition, student affairs leaders must assist other members of the college community in understanding what matters, why decisions are made, and how resources are allocated or reallocated in the student affairs area.

Know When to Let Go of Programs That Do Not Make a Difference. Student affairs leaders and practitioners must honestly and objectively analyze data on program effectiveness. If a program—whether it is new or ten years old—does not contribute significantly to student learning and success, its resources must be reallocated. If student affairs practitioners are losing opportunities to create new programs because the department's budget is tied up in legacy programs that generate marginal results, all or part of the resources that support these programs must be reassigned. Both student affairs leaders and practitioners must be able to let go of programs and services that do not contribute in meaningful and measurable ways to student learning and success.

Prepare Practitioners for the Future. A common concern of student affairs practitioners at all levels is that community colleges do not help them acquire the skills to implement new programs or strengthen existing ones (Culp, 2001). Because carefully crafted strategic plans will fail if practitioners lack the skills to implement them, student affairs leaders must work with practitioners to assess their current skill levels, define the skills they need to implement the division's strategic plan, and identify strategies that will allow them to acquire these skills. Although practitioners working in various student affairs areas (advising, assessment, admissions, counseling, financial aid, and student life, for example) do not need identical skill sets, they do need annual *professional development plans* that identify the skills they must acquire in the coming year, outline how they will acquire these skills (through in-service training, on-campus workshops, credit courses, mentoring, or at state or national conferences), and describe the link between the new skills and the student affairs division's strategic plan.

Communicate and Celebrate. Ask anyone on campus if the college could function without faculty and the answer would be a resounding, "Absolutely not." Ask the same question about student affairs divisions, and the answer in many cases would be, "I'm not sure." Senior student affairs officers have an obligation to open lines of communication with every member of the college community—via weekly e-mails, a monthly newsletter, or a quarterly report—to educate them about their programs and services and their contributions to the institution. Student affairs practitioners must intentionally and continually educate their colleagues across the college about their mission, goals, and contributions. And everyone needs to celebrate successes and recognize the people, whether in student affairs divisions or the wider college community, who made these successes possible.

Conclusion

Community colleges have always evolved in response to environmental shifts and increased internal and external expectations, but the changes now come more quickly and with more variety than at any time since the early days of the community college movement (O'Banion, 2004). Eventually, these changes may threaten the existence of student affairs divisions that rely on anecdotal evidence to demonstrate their effectiveness, cling to outdated programs and services, or fail to update their practitioners' skill sets. At the moment, however, these changes present significant opportunities for student affairs practitioners, especially those who understand that the core values of their profession are the core values of any learning-centered institution.

In response to demands for accountability, quality, and the need for learning-centered institutions, many community colleges are in the process of redefining themselves. By implementing cultures of evidence, offering programs that matter to the community college's core mission, updating their knowledge base and skill sets, and helping their faculty colleagues create campus climates that support student learning and success, student affairs practitioners will contribute significantly to this institutional regeneration and demonstrate that strong student affairs programs are essential to the success of the community college. More importantly, these actions will send an important message to the college community: student affairs practitioners have a positive vision of the future, a willingness to acquire the skills to design that future, and the courage to implement data-based programs and services to make that future happen.

References

Astin, A. *What Matters in College.* San Francisco: Jossey-Bass, 1993.
Culp, M. M. "Managing Change Without Destroying Staff, Students, or Student Affairs." Paper presented at the American College Personnel Association convention, Boston, Mar. 2001.
O'Banion, T. *A Learning College for the 21st Century.* Washington, D.C.: American Council on Education and Oryx Press, 1997.

O'Banion, T. "Toward the Future Vitality of Student Development: Refining the Legacy." Paper presented at the National Council on Student Development annual conference, Orlando, Fla., Oct. 2004.

Rogers, C. *On Becoming a Person.* Boston: Houghton Mifflin, 1961.

MARGUERITE M. CULP, formerly senior student affairs officer at Austin Community College in Texas, is now executive director of Solutions-Oriented Consulting in Florida.

7

*This chapter, aimed at both new community college
student affairs professionals and experienced
practitioners hoping to further develop their skills,
provides resources and information about the expanding
focus on student learning, translating student
development theory into practice, and assessing student
learning outcomes.*

Key Resources for Student Affairs
Professionals in Learning-Centered
Community Colleges

Carrie B. Kisker

As publicly funded, open-access institutions, community colleges face myr-
iad demands and expectations—from students, governing bodies, local communities, state and federal politicians, and accrediting agencies. Student
affairs administrators are not insulated from these pressures, and are
increasingly asked to demonstrate their contributions to student learning
and verify the cost-effectiveness of student-oriented programs and services.
As this volume repeatedly demonstrates, community college student affairs
professionals must respond to these demands by identifying essential programs and services on their campuses, assessing and evaluating them appropriately, and finally, allocating human and financial resources to those that
truly contribute to student learning.

Despite understanding the importance of focusing on what really matters, many community college student affairs professionals may not possess
the requisite knowledge to implement practices based explicitly on college
student development or learning theory, let alone the skills they need to
assess and evaluate program effectiveness. Indeed, there is a vast diversity
of educational backgrounds among community college student affairs staff.
Some have been trained as counselors, but graduate programs in counseling do not always focus primarily on institutions of higher education, much
less community colleges with their unique missions, challenges, and expectations. In addition, many entry-level student affairs positions do not require
a master's degree; community colleges frequently hire bright, young college
graduates who, despite their enthusiasm and willingness to learn, have had

little exposure to the core values and theories that drive the profession. As well, since the early 1970s, some community colleges have begun replacing counselors and other student affairs staff with paraprofessionals (Hallberg and Associates, 1972); at a minimum, this contributes to the wide variety of educational backgrounds and levels of experience among student affairs practitioners.

Although this diversity of prior experience and training is often touted as a strength of the broader field of student affairs, it may also pose a problem for community college leaders who—in order to respond to both internal and external demands and expectations—rely on student affairs professionals to demonstrate the essential connections between student affairs practice and student learning, assess students as they progress through the college, and evaluate programs and services for both programmatic effectiveness and cost-effectiveness.

This chapter focuses on three important themes discussed throughout this volume: the expanding focus on student learning, applying student development theory to practice, and assessing student affairs programs and services. New student affairs professionals in the community college, as well as experienced practitioners hoping to update their skills, can use the information and resources presented here to effectively implement learning-centered practices on their campuses. Most of the resources highlighted in this chapter are available through the ERIC database at http://www.eric.ed.gov, and many more can be accessed online or at a local college or university library.

Expanding Focus on Student Learning

For many years, the concept of student development—progress through identifiable cognitive, ethical, or affective stages—was the underpinning of the student affairs profession (see Chapter One in this volume). Although this focus has not gone away, many student affairs scholars and administrators have more recently begun to call attention to student learning as the central purpose of the profession. This shift in emphasis is especially relevant at two-year colleges that enroll students of all ages, from all walks of life, and in all stages of intellectual, emotional, and moral development. The following resources provide student affairs practitioners new to the community college, as well as those interested in learning more about this topic, with information on how student affairs practice fits into the idea of the two-year college as a learning-centered institution.

O'Banion, T. *A Learning College for the 21st Century*. Washington, D.C.: American Council on Education and Oryx Press, 1997.

Terry O'Banion, president emeritus of the League for Innovation in the Community College, is widely credited with the now-popular notion that the community college, at its core, is a learning and learner-centered institution. In this book, O'Banion reviews the emerging emphasis on learning in higher education and the development of the concept of learning colleges. Several contributing authors provide specific case studies of reform efforts at community colleges, and the book concludes with a practical guide for community college faculty, staff, and administrators interested in refocusing their campuses around the concept of student learning.

Whitt, E. J. (ed.). *Student Learning as Student Affairs Work: Responding to Our Imperative.* NASPA Monograph Series 23. Washington, D.C.: National Association of Student Personnel Administrators, 1999.

This monograph centers on five key questions: (1) How can student affairs programs and services evolve to become more learning-centered? (2) In what ways do common student affairs expectations, assumptions, and practices inhibit or foster student learning? (3) How can student affairs professionals form successful partnerships with their academic colleagues to promote student learning? (4) How do we know students are learning? (5) What knowledge and skills must student affairs practitioners possess in order to foster student learning? Chapter authors explore these five questions in depth and describe actions that student affairs staff can take to implement the student learning imperative.

Dale, P., and Shoenhair, C. "Learning-Centered Practices in Student Services." Phoenix, Ariz.: Paradise Valley Community College, 2000. (ED 445 732)

This descriptive report identifies characteristics of learning-centered student services on community college campuses. Among others, these best practices include engaging students in active learning, identifying and evaluating learning outcomes, linking budget allocations to learning objectives, building inclusive and supportive learning environments, and offering services to students any time and any place. The authors acknowledge that not all student service areas will implement learning-centered practices in the same way or at the same rate, and offer a list of criteria by which student affairs practitioners can measure their progress toward becoming more learning-centered.

Williams, T. E. "Challenges in Supporting Student Learning and Success Through Student Services." In T. H. Bers and H. D. Calhoun (eds.), *Next Steps for the Community College.* New Directions for Community Colleges, no. 117. San Francisco: Jossey-Bass, 2002.

This *New Directions for Community Colleges* chapter identifies challenges facing student affairs practitioners in the two-year college, including the focus on supporting student learning. Williams argues that it is important to emphasize both student learning and student success, because many community college students are more interested in the tangible outcomes of an education than in the actual process of learning. The chapter also provides examples of programs and services at community colleges across the country that effectively promote student learning and success.

Applying Student Development Theory to Practice

Although documenting student learning has recently become a focus in student affairs offices across the country, the profession has not abandoned its core mandate to "assist the student in developing to the limits of his potentialities" (American Council on Education, 1983, p. 3). Yet community college student affairs practitioners who have not taken graduate courses in higher education administration or counseling, or whose previous experience or training was with primary or secondary school students, may not be familiar with the student development theories that guide the profession or with the ways in which theory can be applied to practice. The first four publications listed in this section detail three significant student development theories; the last three provide student affairs practitioners with information and advice on applying theory to practice.

Chickering, A. W., and Reisser, L. *Education and Identity* (2nd ed.). San Francisco: Jossey-Bass, 1993.

In 1969, Arthur Chickering identified seven vectors of college student development: achieving competence, managing emotions, developing autonomy, establishing identity, freeing interpersonal relationships, clarifying purpose, and developing integrity. Despite its popularity, several researchers have questioned how applicable Chickering's original model was to non-white, nontraditional age community college students. This book, written by Chickering and Reisser, demonstrates that many of the seven vectors also apply to older students who are developing new competencies and reexamining their sense of identity and purpose. As Higbee, Arendale, and Lundell (2005) note, Chickering's seven vectors "can be particularly useful in identifying the competing demands on community college students' time and in demonstrating that development can occur simultaneously in many aspects of students' lives" (p. 6).

Perry, W. G. *Forms of Intellectual and Ethical Development in the College Years: A Scheme.* Austin, Tex.: Holt, Reinhart and Winston, 1970.

This book outlines the author's scheme of ethical and intellectual development in college students. According to Perry, when students enter college they are likely to view the world from a dualistic perspective in which answers are either right or wrong and in which authority figures are usually believed to know best. As they develop, they gain a more complex, relativistic view of the world and of themselves. This scheme is especially important to student affairs professionals because it demonstrates that the *processes* involved in students' intellectual and ethical development are as important as the content or outcomes of that development.

Astin, A. W. "Student Involvement: A Developmental Theory for Higher Education." *Journal of College Student Personnel,* 1984, *25,* 297–308. http://www.findarticles.com/p/articles/mi_qa3752/is_199909/ai_n8859160. Accessed Apr. 22, 2005.

Astin's theory of student involvement has greatly influenced the field of student affairs. The two key tenets of this theory are that (1) "the amount of student learning and personal development associated with any educational program is directly proportional to the quality and quantity of student involvement in that program," and (2) "the effectiveness of any educational policy or practice is directly related to the capacity of that policy or practice to increase student involvement" (n.p.). Although this theory has been criticized for focusing on four-year college students rather than those attending community colleges, this relatively straightforward theory both reinforces the value of student affairs programs and services and provides guidance for practitioners working to enhance student success.

Gilligan, C. *In a Different Voice: Psychological Theory and Women's Development* (2nd ed.). Cambridge, Mass.: Harvard University Press, 1993.

Although highly influential, many student development theorists (including Chickering, Perry, and Astin) have been criticized for developing their theories based on examinations of a relatively homogeneous population (often young white males). When these theories are generalized to a more diverse student body, there is a danger that people who develop differently (for example, women and people of color) may be perceived as inferior. In this book, Gilligan proposes a stage theory of moral development for women in order to assert that women are not inferior in their personal or moral development but, rather, are different. Women develop in a way that focuses on creating connections among people and with an ethic of care, as opposed to an ethic of justice.

National Council on Student Development. "Toward the Future Vitality of Student Development Services: Redefining the Legacy in 2004." Transcript of a colloquium at the National Council on Student Development annual conference, Orlando, Fla., Oct. 2004.

The National Council on Student Development (NCSD) is the only national organization that exclusively represents student development professionals at two-year colleges. In 2004, NCSD held a colloquium on the future of student development in the community college. This colloquium celebrated the 20th anniversary of one held in 1984, out of which came what is commonly known as the 1984 *Traverse City Statement* (Keyser, 1984), a seminal document on community college student development. As part of this celebration, participants at the 2004 colloquium produced *Toward the Future Vitality of Student Development Services: Redefining the Legacy in 2004,* better known as the 2004 *Traverse City Statement.* This document contains recommendations for student affairs professionals concerned about the role of student development and counseling in the community college, learner expectations, enrollment management and student persistence, and helping underprepared students succeed. Draft versions of the 2004 statement are currently available to NCSD members at http://www.NCSDonline.org.

Wimbish, J., Bumphus, W., and Helfgot, S. R. "Evolving Theory, Informing Practice." In S. R. Helfgot and M. M. Culp (eds.), *Promoting Student Success in Community Colleges.* New Directions for Student Services, no. 69. San Francisco: Jossey-Bass, 1995.

This *New Directions for Student Services* chapter offers a historical analysis of the relationship between student affairs theory and practice, and it examines both traditional and more recent student development theories. The chapter also gives examples of community college programs that have emerged from these theories, as well as a list of sources that community college student affairs professionals might find useful as they attempt to use theory to inform practice on their own campus.

Dassance, C. R., and Harr, G. "Student Development from Theory to Practice." In W. L. Deegan and T. O'Banion (eds.), *Perspectives on Student Development.* New Directions for Community Colleges, no. 67. San Francisco: Jossey-Bass, 1989.

Although they note that applying student development theory to practice can sometimes be difficult, Dassance and Harr argue that this is not an acceptable reason for abandoning the effort. As this chapter demonstrates, when theory is supplemented with an appreciation for the local context in which student development occurs, when strong, effective leadership and support is evident, and when student affairs practitioners effectively and ethically apply strategies and tactics to "optimize the possibility for success" (p. 26), student development theory can successfully inform student affairs practice.

Assessing Student Learning Outcomes

According to Friedlander and Serban (2004), one of the greatest challenges in assessing student learning outcomes in community colleges is the lack of knowledge about assessment processes, models, and tools. As they note, few administrators, faculty, and staff have been formally trained in identifying valid and measurable learning outcomes, and even fewer know how to develop assessment questions, methods, or instruments. Furthermore, few colleges have the requisite infrastructure or the extra funding to support large-scale professional development for student affairs practitioners seeking the knowledge and skills necessary to assess and evaluate student programs and services effectively. Yet as contributors to this volume repeatedly argue, building a culture of evidence is imperative if student affairs professionals are to successfully demonstrate their contributions to student learning (see Chapter Two in this volume). The following resources provide new community college student affairs practitioners, as well as those hoping to update their skills, with information and strategies for assessing student support programs and services.

Morante, E. A. "Assessing Student Services and Academic Support Services." *IJournal, Insight into Student Services*, 2003, 4. (ED 481 834) http://www.ijournal.us/issue_04/ij_issue04_EdwardMorante_01.htm. Accessed Apr. 14, 2005.

This article provides an overview of ways student and academic affairs administrators can initiate a comprehensive and effective assessment program, and outlines three key questions educators must answer in order to assess student learning effectively. First, what are students expected to learn? Second, how will students be able to demonstrate that they have learned what they are expected to learn? Third, how will assessment results be used to improve student learning? The article concludes by offering suggestions to help student affairs professionals effectively implement assessment programs on their campus. Student affairs practitioners might also find useful Morante's *Handbook on Outcomes Assessment for Two-Year Colleges* (2003).

Schuh, J. H., and Upcraft, M. L. *Assessment Practice in Student Affairs: An Applications Manual*. San Francisco: Jossey-Bass, 2000.

This book, a sequel to *Assessment in Student Affairs: A Guide for Practitioners* (Upcraft and Schuh, 1996), describes assessment tools, details different assessment methodologies, approaches, and challenges, and provides a step-by-step approach for implementing effective student affairs assessments at community and four-year colleges. The book pays particular attention to the importance of cost-effectiveness in program assessment.

Weinstein, D. A. "Assessing Student Services Outcomes in the Community College." *Journal of Applied Research in the Community College*, 2002, 9(2), 125–130.

This article describes the philosophy behind outcomes assessment in community college student services and provides practical steps for implementing assessment of student learning outcomes. Weinstein discusses several assessment models, and pays particular attention to Nichols's outcomes assessment template (1995). In addition, this article describes the processes involved in implementing student services outcomes assessment at Lower Columbia College, a two-year college in the state of Washington.

Winston, R. B. Jr., and Miller, T. K. "A Model for Assessing Developmental Outcomes Related to Student Affairs Programs and Services." *NASPA Journal*, 1994, 32(1), 2–19.

In this article, Winston and Miller outline a model for assessing the effects of student affairs programs and services on student development outcomes. Specifically, the authors examine how programs, services, and environmental interventions work individually and in tandem to promote and support students' developmental processes. The article includes practical suggestions and a ten-step process for program implementation based on this model, and discusses the political considerations inherent in implementing new evaluation programs. Although this article focuses primarily on student affairs programs and services in four-year colleges, many of its findings and suggestions are also applicable to the community college.

Conclusion

The books and articles listed in this chapter are but a few examples of the many resources available to student affairs professionals to assist them in learning more about implementing and evaluating cost-effective programs and practices that support student learning. Student affairs associations such as the National Association of Student Personnel Administrators and the American College Personnel Association can provide community college practitioners with useful information about effective programs and best practices, and are helpful vehicles for connecting with other professionals across the country.

In addition, the ERIC database (http://www.eric.ed.gov) contains many single-institution reports and unpublished best practice examples that can provide excellent advice and guidance for community college student affairs personnel. Finally, college-based professional development initiatives can be valuable in helping student affairs practitioners learn about the core values and theories in their field, as well as issues related to assessment and evaluation. All of these resources can assist student affairs practitioners, who arrive at the community college through diverse educational and experiential pathways, in gaining the background knowledge and skills they need to implement those programs and practices that truly contribute to student learning and development.

References

American Council on Education. "The Student Personnel Point of View." In G. T. Saddlemire and A. L. Rents (eds.), *Student Affairs: A Profession's Heritage: Significant Articles, Authors, Issues, and Documents.* Carbondale, Ill.: American College Personnel Association, 1983.

Chickering, A. W. *Education and Identity.* San Francisco: Jossey-Bass, 1969.

Friedlander, J., and Serban, A. M. "Meeting the Challenges of Assessing Student Learning Outcomes." In A. M. Serban and J. Friedlander (eds.), *Developing and Implementing Assessment of Student Learning Outcomes.* New Directions for Community Colleges, no. 126. San Francisco: Jossey-Bass, 2004.

Hallberg, E. C., and Associates. "Paraprofessionals . . . As Counselors." *Community and Junior College Journal,* 1972, 43(2), 30–31.

Higbee, J. L., Arendale, D. R., and Lundell, D. B. "Using Theory and Research to Improve Access and Retention in Developmental Education." In C. Kozeracki (ed.), *Responding to the Challenges of Developmental Education.* New Directions for Community Colleges, no. 129. San Francisco: Jossey-Bass, 2005.

Keyser, J. S. (ed.). *Traverse City Statement: Toward the Future Vitality of Student Development Services.* Iowa City: American College Testing Program, 1984.

Morante, E. A. *A Handbook on Outcomes Assessment for Two-Year Colleges.* Palm Desert, Calif.: College of the Desert and California Community College Fund for Instructional Improvement, 2003. (ED 482 595) http://www.collegeofthedesert.edu/uploadedFiles/AssessmentHandbookSpring03(1).pdf. Accessed Apr. 14, 2005.

Nichols, J. O. *The Departmental Guide and Record Book for Student Outcomes Assessment and Institutional Effectiveness.* Edison, N.J.: Agathon, 1995.

Upcraft, M. L., and Schuh, J. H. *Assessment in Student Affairs: A Guide for Practitioners.* San Francisco: Jossey-Bass, 1996.

CARRIE B. KISKER is managing editor of the New Directions for Community Colleges series and a doctoral student in higher education at the University of California, Los Angeles.

Appendix: Results of a National Survey Identifying Challenges and Opportunities for Student Affairs

Background Information
Surveys distributed: 210
Recipients: presidents and senior student affairs officers belonging to the
  League for Innovation in the Community College, American Association
  of Community College Governing Boards, and Lumina institutions, as
  well as ACPA, NASPA, and NCSD leaders
Surveys completed: 75, for a 35.7 percent response rate
Note: Numbers in following tables do not always total 75 because not all
  respondents answered all questions.

Demographic Picture of Respondents
Type of institution: urban (28), suburban (23), rural (13), no response (11)
Location: Northeast (9), Northwest (6), Southwest (16), West (5), Midwest
  (21), Southeast (14), South (1), no response (3)
Total student enrollment: Under 5,000 (15), 5,001–10,000 (19), 10,001–
  20,000 (14), 20,001–30,000 (11), 30,000+ (13), no response (3)
Respondent position: president (19), vice president (27), chancellor (2), vice
  chancellor (1), dean (20), director (4), no response (2)

Configuration of Student Affairs at Respondents' Institutions
Stand-alone: 63
Combined with other area: 12 (6 with academic affairs, 1 with community
  affairs, 1 with learning support, 1 with technology, marketing, off-campus
  centers, and the library; another 3 were broken up and assigned by function to various areas in the college)

Titles of Persons Viewed as Senior Student Affairs Officer

Vice Chancellor; EVP for Academic and Student Affairs (3); VP for Student Services (13); VP for Student Development (6); VP for Enrollment and Student Services (2); VP for Student Affairs (4); VP (2); VP for Educational Services; VP for Academic and Student Affairs; VP for Learning Support; VP for Student Affairs and Enrollment Management (2); VP for Student Development and Success; VP for Student Development Services (2); VP for Student Development and a VP for Enrollment Services (one college); VP for Student and Education Services; VP for Instruction; Associate Vice President, Retention and Student Services; Provost for Education Executive Dean, Learning Support Services; Executive Dean for Student Enrollment and Development; Executive Dean for Student Support Services; Executive Dean of the Campus and Student Services; Dean of Students/ Student Services or Student Affairs (17); Dean or Director of Enrollment Services (2); Dean of Enrollment and Student Development; Dean of Student Development and Educational Services; Dean of Student Services and Enrollment Management; Dean of Student Support Services; Dean of Learning Support Services; Director of Student Services

Person to Whom Senior Student Affairs Officer Reports

Chancellor or president: 64 (85%)
EVP, vice chancellor, or provost: 7 (9%)
VP for instruction/instructional services: 2 (3%)
No response: 2 (3%)

Comments from Chancellors, Presidents, Vice Presidents, and Deans Who Believe the Role of Student Affairs Will Increase

Chancellors and presidents agree that student affairs professionals are inextricably linked to instruction and student success, and predict that demands for accountability, the influx of first-generation students, and the increase in students unprepared to benefit from college will strengthen that link. However, chancellors and presidents challenge student affairs professionals to demonstrate that they effectively use the resources allocated to them, offer programs and services that the college needs instead of programs and services that professionals want to provide, and add value to the institution's core mission. In addition, presidents want to see student affairs personnel become more involved in supporting online learners, dual enrollment high school students, and at-risk students.

Vice presidents believe that student affairs professionals are "at the table in a much more substantive way" due to the emphasis on student learning, student success, and student learning outcomes. Vice presidents are concerned about the cost of responding to mental health and social welfare issues, providing accommodations to students with disabilities, and meeting the needs of English-as-a-Second Language students. Although vice

Projected Change in the Role of Student Affairs at Your Institution in the Next Five to Ten Years, by Respondent Position

	Increase	Decrease	Stay Same	Don't Know
Chancellor, vice chancellor	3 (100%)			
President	15 (79%)		4 (21%)	
Vice president	18 (64%)	2 (7%)	7 (25%)	1 (4%)
Dean	13 (68%)	1 (5%)	5 (26%)	
Director	4 (100%)			
Title not given	2 (100%)			
Total	55 (73%)	3 (4%)	16 (21%)	1 (1%)

presidents believe that technology will play an important role in meeting student and institutional demands, they do not see it solving all of the problems facing the profession.

Deans share the vice presidents' perceptions that student affairs programs and services are essential to the community college. Deans understand the mandate to design programs and services that meet the needs of an increasingly diverse student population as well as the needs of new faculty members entering the community college in the next decade. In addition, deans value partnerships with their academic colleagues and welcome the opportunity to become more involved with enrollment management, student retention, faculty mentoring, assessment, and educational planning.

Comments from Chancellors, Presidents, Vice Presidents, and Deans Who Believe the Role of Student Affairs Will Decline

Chancellors, presidents, vice presidents, and deans who believe the role of student affairs in the community college will decline cite three reasons: the constant battle for funding and recognition, the emphasis on student development rather than the customer service models of business and industry, and leadership changes that increase the influence of academic affairs at the expense of student affairs.

Comments from Chancellors, Presidents, Vice Presidents, and Deans Who Believe the Role of Student Affairs Will Stay the Same

One president spoke for all respondents in this category when he wrote, "Student affairs is a vital part of the college and I don't think that will change over time; the way in which services are delivered may change and the mix of services may change, but there will be a significant role to be played."

Major Challenges to the Institution

	Major Challenge That Could Threaten Institution and Student Affairs (percent)	Secondary Challenge That Could Change How Student Affairs Does Business (percent)	Minor Challenge That May Require Resource Reallocation (percent)
Lack of stability in resources or funding	37 (49%)	18 (24%)	7 (9%)
Focus on student learning and student success	20 (27%)	30 (40%)	12 (16%)
Enrollment growth or fluctuations	18 (24%)	31 (41%)	15 (20%)
Building and maintaining academic affairs and student affairs relationships	14 (19%)	24 (32%)	18 (24%)
Legislative initiatives	14 (19%)	23 (31%)	18 (24%)
Building and maintaining relationships with legislators	13 (17%)	17 (23%)	17 (23%)
Shifting demographics	13 (17%)	28 (37%)	21 (28%)
Increasing or changing community expectations	13 (17%)	18 (23%)	28 (39%)
Staffing issues (aging staff or recruiting new staff)	13 (16%)	26 (35%)	20 (27%)
Engaging and involving students, especially with student services	12 (16%)	29 (39%)	23 (31%)
Increasing accountability and need to quantify results	10 (13%)	41 (55%)	13 (16%)
Maintaining the identity of student affairs	8 (11%)	16 (21%)	15 (20%)
Building and maintaining relationships with external communities	5 (7%)	20 (27%)	29 (39%)

Rank Ordering of the Importance of Major Challenges to the Institution

Rank	1	2	3	4	5	6	7	8	9	10	11	12	13	14
Student learning and student success	26	4	7	8	4	3			1	4		1		
Lack of stability in resources or funding	15	8	1	2	3	3	5	1	2	1	2	3	1	
Enrollment growth or fluctuations	7	11	4	9	6	2	4	5	3	3	3	1		2
Building and maintaining effective relationships with academic affairs	5	4	4	4	6	7	4	4	6	7	4	2	2	
Shifting demographics	5	6	7	6	5		7	3	4	1	4	6		
Engaging and involving students	3	9	4	6	6	6	1	9	5	3	4	3		
Building and maintaining effective relationships with external communities	2	1	2	1	5	6	7	5	5	8	5	8	5	1
Increasing accountability or need to justify results	1	7	9	6	7	8	4	3	5	3	3	2	2	
Building and maintaining effective relationships with legislators	1	4	3	1	3	5	8	4	3	2	4	5	11	
Community expectations	1	3	4	2	7	5	1	6	7	4	10	6	1	1
Legislative initiatives	1	2	5	4	2	1	5	5	7	7	6	10	1	3
Staffing issues (aging staff or recruiting new staff)	1	1	4	5	8	9		4	4	4	4	5	3	
Maintaining identity of student affairs	1	1	4	2	1	1	6	2	4	4	7	5	21	

Note: 1 = most important; 14 = least important.

Instruments Used to Measure Student Success
Respondents could check more than one instrument.

	Previously	Currently
Community College Survey of Student Engagement	12	29
Noel-Levitz	22	27
National Benchmarking Project	9	13
Local instrument: student learning	12	45
Local instrument: student success	12	42
Local instrument: student engagement	12	28
Other (student, alumni, or employer satisfaction, senior college data, Title III criteria, CUNY student satisfaction survey, QCC student satisfaction survey learning outcomes, and so forth)	0	15

Most Important Measures of or Criteria for Student Success at Respondents' Institutions
This was an open-ended question.
The following were identified by fifteen or more respondents:

- Graduation and transfer rates (43)
- Retention rates (29)
- Achievement of goals and objectives (26)
- Job placement (18)

The following were identified by five to fourteen respondents:

- Student satisfaction (13)
- GPA (11)
- GPA, successful performance at the university (11)
- Course completion rates (7)
- Course competency rates (6)
- Learning outcomes (5)

The following were identified by two to four respondents:

- Licensure and certification exams (4)
- Student engagement (3)
- Employer evaluation of graduates (2)
- Research studies (2)
- Success of students in developmental courses (2)
- Self-assessment (2)
- Student growth (2)
- Success in "gateway" courses (2)

What Would Most Strengthen Student Affairs at Your Institution?

The following is a sample of responses to the above open-ended question; responses are sorted by position.

Chancellors, vice chancellors, and presidents stated the following:

- Better data collection, planning, evaluation, and understanding of the services students need (7)
- More extensive staff development (7)
- Additional funding and staff (6)
- More collaboration with academic affairs (5)
- Improved understanding of the value of student affairs (4)
- More consistency, depth, teamwork, and professionalism (3)
- More effective and visionary leadership (2)
- Improved facilities (2)
- Increased emphasis on student success (2)
- Stronger presence in the community (2)

Vice presidents stated the following:

- Additional funding, especially for accommodations, financial aid, retention initiatives, and student activities (13)
- More collaboration and communication between academic affairs and student affairs (10)
- Additional staff (8)
- Staff development for all, and leadership training for new professionals (5)
- More support from the chancellor or president (4)
- New or improved facilities (3)
- More opportunities for students to receive leadership training, participate in clubs, and have a voice in institutional governance (3)
- Stronger leadership within student affairs (3)

Deans and directors stated the following:

- Additional funding (6)
- More collaboration with instructional personnel (6)
- Additional staffing (5)
- Additional resources (3)
- More professional development (4)
- More cross-training opportunities (3)
- Better understanding and use of assessment (3)
- Better understanding and use of technology (2)

- Better facilities (2)
- Increased multicultural competence among staff members (2)
- Greater focus on the college's mission, obtaining better-qualified staff, and establishing closer connections to area schools (2)
- More mandatory programs for students, such as orientation and placement (2)

INDEX

Back Issue/Subscription Order Form

Copy or detach and send to:
Jossey-Bass, A Wiley Imprint, 989 Market Street, San Francisco CA 94103-1741

Call or fax toll-free: Phone 888-378-2537 6:30AM – 3PM PST; Fax 888-481-2665

Back Issues: Please send me the following issues at $29 each
(Important: please include ISBN number with your order.)

_____

_____

_____

$ _____   Total for single issues

$ _____   SHIPPING CHARGES: SURFACE   Domestic Canadian
                                    First Item $5.00 $6.00
                                    Each Add'l Item $3.00 $1.50
                 For next-day and second-day delivery rates, call the number listed above.

Subscriptions   Please __ start __ renew my subscription to *New Directions for Community Colleges* for the year 2____at the following rate:

U.S.   __ Individual $80   __ Institutional $170
Canada   __ Individual $80   __ Institutional $210
All Others   __ Individual $104   __ Institutional $244
Online subscriptions are available too!

For more information about online subscriptions visit www.interscience.wiley.com

$ _____   Total single issues and subscriptions (Add appropriate sales tax for your state for single issue orders. No sales tax for U.S. subscriptions. Canadian residents, add GST for subscriptions and single issues.)

__Payment enclosed (U.S. check or money order only)
__VISA __ MC __ AmEx __ # _____Exp. Date _____

Signature _____ Day Phone _____
__ Bill Me (U.S. institutional orders only. Purchase order required.)

Purchase order # _____
                 Federal Tax ID13559302   **GST 89102 8052**

Name _____

Address _____

_____

Phone _____ E-mail _____

For more information about Jossey-Bass, visit our Web site at www.josseybass.com

CC126 **Developing and Implementing Assessment of Student Learning Outcomes**
Andreea M. Serban, Jack Friedlander
Colleges are under increasing pressure to produce evidence of student
learning, but most assessment research focuses on four-year colleges. This
volume is designed for practitioners looking for models that community
colleges can apply to measuring student learning outcomes at the classroom,
course, program, and institutional levels to satisfy legislative and
accreditation requirements.
ISBN: 0-7879-7687-3

CC125 **Legal Issues in the Community College**
Robert C. Cloud
Community colleges must be prepared for lawsuits, federal statutes, court
rulings, union negotiations, and other legal issues that could affect
institutional stability and effectiveness. This volume provides leaders with
information about board relations, tenure and employment, student rights
and safety, disability law, risk management, copyright and technology
issues, and more.
ISBN: 0-7879-7482-X

CC124 **Successful Approaches to Fundraising and Development**
Mark David Milliron, Gerardo E. de los Santos, Boo Browning
This volume outlines how community colleges can tap into financial support
from the private sector, as four-year institutions have been doing. Chapter
authors discuss building community college foundations, cultivating
relationships with the local community, generating new sources of revenue,
fundraising from alumni, and the roles of boards, presidents, and trustees.
ISBN: 0-7879-7283-5

CC123 **Help Wanted: Preparing Community College Leaders in a New Century**
William E. Piland, David B. Wolf
This issue brings together various thoughtful perspectives on the nature of
leading community colleges over the foreseeable future. Authors offer
suggestions for specific programmatic actions that community colleges
themselves can take to provide the quantity, quality, specializations, and
diversity of leaders that are needed.
ISBN: 0-7879-7248-7

CC122 **Classification Systems for Two-Year Colleges**
Alexander C. McCormick, Rebecca D. Cox
This critically important volume advances the conversation among
researchers and practitioners about possible approaches to classifying two-
year colleges. After an introduction to the history, purpose, practice, and
pitfalls of classifying colleges and universities, five different classification
schemes are presented, followed by commentary by knowledgable
respondents representing potential users of a classification system:
community college associations, institutional leaders, and researchers. The
final chapter applies the five proposed schemes to a sample of colleges for
purposes of illustration.
ISBN: 0-7879-7171-5

CC121 The Role of the Community College in Teacher Education
Barbara K. Townsend, Jan M. Ignash
Illustrates the extent to which community colleges have become major
players in teacher education, not only in the traditional way of providing the
first two years of an undergraduate degree in teacher education but in more
controversial ways such as offering associate and baccalaureate degrees in
teacher education and providing alternative certification programs.
ISBN: 0-7879-6868-4

CC120 Enhancing Community Colleges Through Professional Development
Gordon E. Watts
Offers a much needed perspective on the expanding role of professional
development in community colleges. Chapter authors provide descriptions
of how their institutions have addressed issues through professional
development, created institutional change, developed new delivery systems
for professional development, reached beyond development just for faculty,
and found new uses for traditional development activities.
ISBN: 0-7879-6330-5

CC119 Developing Successful Partnerships with Business and the Community
Mary S. Spangler
Demonstrates that there are many different approaches to community
colleges' partnering with the private sector and that when partners are
actively engaged in tailoring education, training, and learning to their
students, everyone is the beneficiary.
ISBN: 0-7879-6321-9

CC118 Community College Faculty: Characteristics, Practices, and Challenges
Charles Outcalt
Offers multiple perspectives on the ways community college faculty fulfill
their complex professional roles. With data from national surveys, this
volume provides an overview of community college faculty, looks at their
primary teaching responsibility, and examines particular groups of
instructors, including part-timers, women, and people of color.
ISBN: 0-7879-6328-3

CC117 Next Steps for the Community College
Trudy H. Bers, Harriott D. Calhoun
Provides an overview of relevant literature and practice covering major
community college topics: transfer rates, vocational education, remedial
and developmental education, English as a second language education,
assessment of student learning, student services, faculty and staff, and
governance and policy. Includes a chapter discussing the categories,
types, and purposes of literature about community colleges and the
major publications germane to community college practitioners and
scholars.
ISBN: 0-7879-6289-9

CC116 The Community College Role in Welfare to Work
C. David Lisman
Provides examples of effective programs including a job placement program
meeting the needs of rural welfare recipients, short-term and advanced levels
of technical training, a call center program for customer service job training,

beneficial postsecondary training, collaborative programs for long-term family economic self-sufficiency, and a family-based approach recognizing the needs of welfare recipients and their families.
ISBN: 0-7879-5781-X

CC115   The New Vocationalism in Community Colleges
Debra D. Bragg
Analyzes the role of community college leaders in developing programs, successful partnerships and collaboration with communities, work-based learning, changes in perception of terminal education and transfer education, changing instructional practices for changing student populations and the integration of vocational education into the broader agenda of American higher education.
ISBN: 0-7879-5780-1

CC114   Transfer Students: Trends and Issues
Frankie Santos Laanan
Evaluates recent research and policy discussions surrounding transfer students, and summarizes three broad themes in transfer policy: re-search, student and academic issues, and institutional factors. Argues that institutions are in a strategic position to provide students with programs for rigorous academic training as well as opportunities to participate in formal articulation agreements with senior institutions.
ISBN: 0-7879-5779-8

CC113   Systems for Offering Concurrent Enrollment at High Schools and Community Colleges
Piedad F. Robertson, Brian G. Chapman, Fred Gaskin
Offers approaches to creating valuable programs, detailing all the components necessary for the success and credibility of concurrent enrollment. Focuses on the faculty liaisons from appropriate disciplines that provide the framework for an ever-improving program.
ISBN: 0-7879-5758-5

CC112   Beyond Access: Methods and Models for Increasing Retention and Learning Among Minority Students
Steven R. Aragon
Presents practical models, alternative approaches and new strategies for creating effective cross-cultural courses that foster higher retention and learning success for minority students. Argues that educational programs must now develop a broader curriculum that includes multicultural and multi-linguistic information.
ISBN: 0-7879-5429-2

CC111   How Community Colleges Can Create Productive Collaborations with Local Schools
James C. Palmer
Details ways that community colleges and high schools can work together to help students navigate the difficult passage from secondary to higher education. Provides detailed case studies of actual collaborations between specific community colleges and high school districts, discuss legal problems that can arise when high school students enroll in community colleges, and more.
ISBN: 0-7879-5428-4

NEW DIRECTIONS FOR COMMUNITY COLLEGES IS NOW AVAILABLE ONLINE AT WILEY INTERSCIENCE

What is Wiley InterScience?

Wiley InterScience is the dynamic online content service from John Wiley & Sons delivering the full text of over 300 leading scientific, technical, medical, and professional journals, plus major reference works, the acclaimed *Current Protocols* laboratory manuals, and even the full text of select Wiley print books online.

What are some special features of Wiley InterScience?

Wiley InterScience Alerts is a service that delivers table of contents via e-mail for any journal available on Wiley InterScience as soon as a new issue is published online.

Early View is Wiley's exclusive service presenting individual articles online as soon as they are ready, even before the release of the compiled print issue. These articles are complete, peer-reviewed, and citable.

CrossRef is the innovative multi-publisher reference linking system enabling readers to move seamlessly from a reference in a journal article to the cited publication, typically located on a different server and published by a different publisher.

How can I access Wiley InterScience?

Visit http://www.interscience.wiley.com

Guest Users can browse Wiley InterScience for unrestricted access to journal Tables of Contents and Article Abstracts, or use the powerful search engine.
Registered Users are provided with a *Personal Home Page* to store and manage customized alerts, searches, and links to favorite journals and articles. Additionally, Registered Users can view free Online Sample Issues and preview selected material from major reference works.
Licensed Customers are entitled to access full-text journal articles in PDF, with select journals also offering full-text HTML.

How do I become an Authorized User?

Authorized Users are individuals authorized by a paying Customer to have access to the journals in Wiley InterScience. For example, a university that subscribes to Wiley journals is considered to be the Customer. Faculty, staff and students authorized by the university to have access to those journals in Wiley InterScience are Authorized Users. Users should contact their Library for information on which Wiley journals they have access to in Wiley InterScience.

ASK YOUR INSTITUTION ABOUT WILEY INTERSCIENCE TODAY!